# Skipper

*Barbie®* Doll's
Little Sister
Second Edition

IDENTIFICATION
& VALUE GUIDE

Also
Featuring
## tutti & todd
BARBIE & SKIPPER'S
TINY TWIN SISTER & BROTHER™

Trina Cottingham,
Scott Arend
& Karla Hemingway
Photography by Barry Sturgill
and Karla Hemingway

COLLECTOR BOOKS
*A Division of Schroeder Publishing Co., Inc.*

Front Cover:
**1968 Twist 'n Turn Skipper
Wearing #1955 Posy Party
NRFB $150.00; M/C $60.00 – 75.00**

Cover design – Terri Hunter
Layout design – Lynda Smith

COLLECTOR BOOKS
P.O. Box 3009
Paducah, Kentucky 42002–3009

www.collectorbooks.com

Copyright © 2011 Trina Cottingham, Scott Arend, Karla Hemingway

The current values in this book should be used only as a guide. They are not intended to set prices, which vary from one section of the country to another. Auction prices as well as dealer prices vary greatly and are affected by condition as well as demand. Neither the authors nor the publisher assumes responsibility for any losses that might be incurred as a result of consulting this guide.

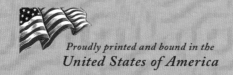

*Proudly printed and bound in the*
*United States of America*

# Contents

# Dedication

This book is dedicated to our moms: Jill Dart Arend, Alana Brandstrom, and Marcia Kent. They started us on the road to collecting many years ago, and without their encouragement, support, and seemingly bottomless checkbooks to assist in purchasing so many of the items photographed, this project would still be unfinished. We love and thank you.

Moms from left to right: Alana Brandstrom, Marcia Kent, and Jill Dart Arend

# Acknowledgments

Our ability to publish this book would not have been possible without the effort and support of so many friends who helped search out missing items, lent us their treasures, tipped us off to rare finds, proofread the manuscript, and provided general assistance in pricing and content. For their invaluable help, we thank:

Shannon Bilawchuk, Michelle Blankenship, Joe Blitman, Leslie Bote, Karen Caviale, Cynthia Chapman, Paul David, Marl Davidson, Stefanie Deutsch, Sarah Sink Eames, Claudia Exinger, Christel Hasibether, Sandi Holder, Jane Sarasohn–Kahn, Franklin Lim Lao, Lisa Mainetti, A. Glenn Mandeville, Barb Mitchell, Jeffrey Moore, Cheryl Nelson, Annette Nott, Cheryl Power, Rosalie Purvis, Barb Roberts, Bradford Samuel, Vicky Scherck, Judy Schizas, Georgia Seibel, Leslie Sena, Carol Spencer, Kitty Stuart, and *Barbie Bazaar* magazine.

A special thanks to Barry Sturgill for his beautiful photographs, the use of many of his dolls, and his artistic input.

For those of you we may have missed or forgotten to list and were a part of this endeavor, we thank you too.

# About the Authors

## Scott Arend

Scott's been collecting vintage Barbie and family dolls since 1986. He was a regular contributor to *Miller's Doll Collector* and *Barbie Bazaar* magazines, and his popular, long–running column, "Scott's Scuttlebutt," was the acknowledged source of new and "secret" Barbie doll information for many years. Scott now spends his time as a personal chef, consulting with restaurants on planning and new menu items, and offers cooking tips and advice online through his blog and website, www.cookwithscott.com.

## Karla Holzerland-Hemingway

A noted collector of vintage Barbie and family dolls since 1985, Karla is well known for her expertise in never-removed-from-box dolls and fashions. Her extensive collection has been frequently used to document articles published about Barbie and family dolls, and she is a noted authority and contributor to online discussions and forums about Barbie and family dolls. In 1993 Karla became the first vintage doll dealer to utilize new telecommunications technology and market dolls via a 900 phone line. In 1999, she built her e-commerce website, www.sissyinseattle.com, selling Christopher Radko ornaments. She sold that business in 2007 to take over her family's real estate firm, Evergreen R/E Group LLC, which she currently owns and operates. She lives with her daughter Sara Kay (7) in Snohomish, Washington. Karla likes to spend her free time training for Ironman Triathalons and Marathons, and just being a mom.

## Trina Cottingham

Trina has been a devoted Skipper doll fan since her "Skipper doll birthday party" in 1981. Trina specializes in licensed and vinyl products, and her mother originally planted the seed to write this book. Her comprehensive Skipper doll collection has been featured in *Barbie Bazaar* magazine to document rare vintage and licensed Skipper doll products. In late 2004 the majority of Trina's Skipper doll collection was stolen and she has enjoyed replacing cherished items since that time. Trina is also an avid collector of vintage Tinkerbell memorabilia, Franciscan dishes, and composition dolls. Since the original printing of this book, Trina married her long-time boyfriend and they have enjoyed 11 years of marriage. Trina lives in Seattle and is a long–time employee of a local nonprofit organization working with children. In her spare time, Trina enjoys creating one–of–a–kind jewelry, knitting, quilting, and working in paper and fiber arts.

# Abbreviations & Values

We have used terminology that is fairly standard in the Barbie doll collecting world to identify and describe the items in this book. They are:

**NRFB/MOC** — never removed from box/mint on card - factory original, not played with

**MIB** — mint in box; removed, but still factory perfect

**Mint** — removed from packaging, but no visible wear or missing pieces

**BL** — bend-leg, bend-leg mechanism

**TNT** — Twist 'n Turn waist, introduced with dolls manufactured from 1967 on

**Mod** — the dolls and outfits manufactured between 1967 and 1972

**M/C** — mint/complete, removed from package, mint, and complete

Some dolls, outfits and accessories that are difficult to find have been graded using a system established by Joe Blitman. In order of increasing rarity, they are:

**HTF** — hard-to-find

**VHTF** — very hard-to-find

**RARE** — rare

**VERY RARE** — next to impossible to find, especially in mint condition

When using the price guide, keep in mind that prices vary from dealer to dealer, and in different geographical locations around the country. We have attempted to list a price range for what you may expect to pay for a NRFB, or mint and complete item. We've sometimes listed a dollar value with a plus sign following — for example $30.00+. In our estimation, you could expect to pay at least $30.00 for the item, but depending on condition, completeness of packaging, and your desire to own the particular piece, you may pay

more. Items and outfits that are missing original pieces, dolls with haircuts, paint flaws, paling, or greening should be discounted according to their problems.

The items listed are at retail price, and reflect what you would probably pay if you tried to replace something that was lost or stolen, even if you originally paid more or less for it. Prices can fluctuate for many reasons, so buy what you like and never pay more for something than you personally think is a fair price. Mattel manufactured these pieces in the tens of thousands, and as a general rule, the items in Skipper dolls' world do not hold as much interest for collectors as Barbie doll.

Most importantly, be an informed buyer, have fun, and expect to meet some great people on your collecting journey.

# Introduction

Mattel's fashion doll, Barbie, was one of the most successful toy lines in history when Skipper, her little sister, was introduced in 1964. Barbie's world of sock hops, soda shops, and fashion modeling was intimidating and foreign to many young children. Mattel created Skipper not only to expand Barbie's world (and increase sales), but also to include the younger child who did not play with Barbie because the doll was too grown up. Here was a doll–sized version of a girl who still loved to skip rope, hold tea parties, and take her doll on outings.

The status of "little sister" often implies a girl whose role is that of back–seat observer to a more glamorous, sophisticated and intelligent older sibling. The younger sister can expect to wear her big sister's hand–me–downs, hear about her scholastic and athletic triumphs, and work harder than ever to move out from under her shadow. But in the case of Skipper, she had her own world of high fashion, fun friends, and important achievements. And, her older sister was one of her very best friends.

In marketing the new Skipper doll, Mattel made a savvy decision to connect her to Barbie doll. Skipper's first ten ensembles were smaller interpretations of well–loved Barbie doll outfits. These "sister fashions" helped entice children to add a Skipper to their collection. In 1965, seven of Skipper doll's 13 new ensembles coordinated with Barbie doll's wardrobe, further establishing a play and consumer buying pattern that Skipper doll was not just a new doll, but one that was needed to complete the family.

It's obvious that Skipper doll was a success, and Mattel had long–range plans for her when she received her first two friends in her second year of production. Her world was rapidly expanding with the inclusion of her own bedroom, and licensed products that included furniture and vehicles for expanded play. By 1966, her clothing no longer imitated Barbie doll's, and she could clearly generate her own sales without the connection to her sister.

Skipper doll and her clothing are often overlooked by the Barbie doll collector as uninteresting because they aren't as glamorous. On closer inspection, many of Skipper's outfits contain equally amusing accessories as well as the beautiful garment detailing usually only associated with Barbie. Beginning in the mid–1960s with her debut, Skipper's wardrobe was well tailored and fairly sophisticated, reflecting the attitude of an era when many young girls wore gloves to school and had matching handbags and hats. As the decade progressed, Carnaby Street influenced the clothing with bright colors, op art prints, patterned tights, bell-bottomed pants, and accessories such as mob caps, granny glasses, and oversized purses.

Mattel continued to make the Skipper doll line fresh and exciting with hairstyle and makeup changes, more posability for the dolls, the inclusion of new friends, and by following current trends. Skipper doll sported the popular "sausage curls" worn by child actresses Anissa Jones of *Family Affair* and Susan Olsen of *The Brady Bunch*. In the 1970s she wore granny dresses, wore overalls, hit the beach in Malibu, participated in the Olympics, and showed her patriotic spirit during the Bicentennial. Whatever a little girl dreamed of doing, Skipper was there to do it with her.

This book chronicles Skipper doll, her ensembles, friends, gift sets, licensed products, and doll cases from her introduction in 1964 through 1978, the last year the first Skipper face mold was used exclusively for the line. We've included as many of the foreign dolls, clothing, and licensed products as we could because the Barbie doll collecting world is global today. With online collecting friendships, the internet, and international doll shows, many unusual Skipper items turn up from other countries that collectors want to know about.

We've also included the world of Tutti and Todd, Barbie and Skipper doll's tiny twin sister and brother. Tutti doll debuted in 1966, with Todd and their friend Chris following in 1967. Although the line only lasted through 1971 in the U.S., it was a huge success in Europe and Canada. Dolls and new outfits continued to be produced for these foreign markets through 1980. A complete catalog of these dolls, ensembles, gift sets, and related products can be found in Chapter 4.

Collection of James Taylor

# Introduction

While we've nearly driven ourselves insane tracking down strange clothing variations and rare dolls, we've undoubtedly missed a few. Mattel produced these items in the thousands, and there are some things that only come to light after the deadline. We'd love to hear about your variation or item that wasn't included in the book, and you may write to us at Karlahemingway@verizon.net.

Many fabric variations are shown. Although we're not sure why these occurred, the factory may have run out of production material and substituted whatever was on hand to meet the quota. Sometimes that might be fabric from another Barbie-related outfit, or something completely different that appears as if a factory worker ran down the road and bought the first bolt of material he came across. The end result is sometimes startling, and variations are usually a great deal of fun to collect.

As for prototypes and samples, a prototype is the first piece created, is unique unto itself, and did not have a clothing label. We refer to samples as anything that has a sample tag, or pieces that were obviously intended as mock-ups of the production version using whatever materials were available. Our intent in including the samples and prototypes was not to confuse or depress collectors that these items were never produced, but to show another facet of Mattel's production process. It also gives us a great opportunity to share these rare treasures and see some of the directions the Skipper line might have taken.

Other than Barbie doll, no other doll in Mattel's line has been in continual production since being introduced. Her longevity indicates that she was a great idea, and kids find her as appealing today as they did in 1964. After reading this book and seeing how charming, zany, whimsical, sweet, and sophisticated Skipper doll, her wardrobe, and her world can be, you'll believe us when we say you really ought to take another look at Skipper.

<u>January 2010</u>
As we prepared this second edition, we were surprised to find we had included "internet collecting" in our original introduction. We have a hard time remembering what internet collecting was like back in 1997, because it has truly changed the hobby since then. Primarily through online auction sites, obscure and rare variations and items have come onto the market like never before. In some cases, this has caused the value of certain items to drop somewhat, while other items have increased in value as collectors have found how incredibly rare certain things actually are. Overall, NRFB items have dropped slightly in value since our first edition, and most items from the 1970s have increased.

We still believe the best advice we can give you when using this book is to collect what you like, and never pay more than what you think is a fair value for the item. There's always another "something" out there, and chances are if you don't get it this time, it will come around again — and that's what the excitement of collecting is all about!

# Chapter 1
# Skipper

# SKIPPER

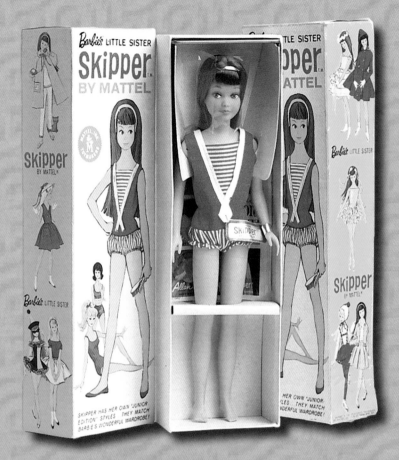

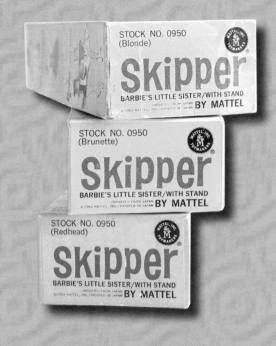

STOCK NO. 0950
(Blonde)
**Skipper**
BARBIE'S LITTLE SISTER/WITH STAND
BY MATTEL

STOCK NO. 0950
(Brunette)
**Skipper**
BARBIE'S LITTLE SISTER/WITH STAND
BY MATTEL

STOCK NO. 0950
(Redhead)
**Skipper**
BARBIE'S LITTLE SISTER/WITH STAND
BY MATTEL

## 0950 – Skipper Doll
## (1964 – 1968)

Barbie doll's little sister Skipper made her debut in 1964 with long, straight hair, solid vinyl legs, and a tan skin tone. She was sold with three distinct hair colors, which were stamped on the box's end flap: blond, brunette, and redhead. Variations within the three main color groups were also produced and include pale lemon blonde, reddish–auburn, coal black (rare), and a "two–tone" brunette hair color. Dolls with the two–tone hair have unusual heavy rooting, using both dark brown and red hair fibers. A very hard–to–find doll, originally rooted with brunette Color Magic hair, has now oxidized to the "carrot–top" orange. From the last half of 1966 through 1968 Skipper doll was sold with pink skin. Skipper doll's accessories included a "gold" wire stand, white comb and brush, red flats, brass headband, swimsuit, and booklet.

Markings:
SKIPPER®
©1963
MATTEL, INC.

**NRFB $195.00 – 225.00**
**M/C $75.00 – 95.00**
**HTF hair colors – $125.00+**

*These are a few examples of the many hair colors available.*

HTF dolls with Color Magic hair and brunette painted scalps.

Photo courtesy of Barry Sturgill

*This unusual doll has two rows of rooted bangs. She is an early Skipper sample doll that belonged to a Mattel employee. The regular issue Skipper doll has only one row of rooted bangs.*

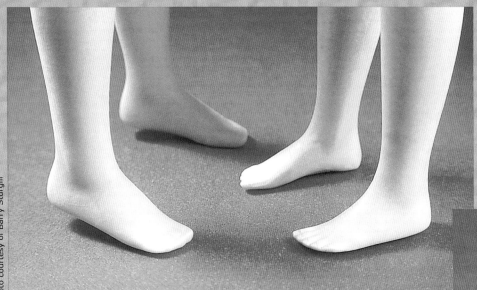

Photo courtesy of Barry Sturgill

*Notice how much larger the sample doll's feet (on left) are than the production issue Skipper doll.*

The first Skipper sample dolls were made of resin and had slightly arched feet with a wider stance.

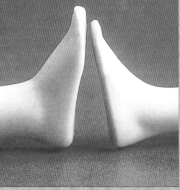

Photo courtesy of Barry Sturgill

Chapter 1

Left – Skipper doll dressed in #1903 Masquerade; right – Skipper doll dressed in #1905 Ballet Class.

Left – Skipper doll dressed in #1904 Flower Girl (Collection of Sandi Holder); right – Skipper doll dressed in #1915 Outdoor Casuals (Collection of Janet Lewis). These two dolls have been reassembled in their boxes incorrectly. They should not have box liners.

## Dressed Box Skipper Dolls (1964 – 1965)

The standard 1964 Skipper doll was also available in several dressed box versions. The box end flap was stamped DRESSED DOLL, and white accent strips were printed between the fashion illustrations on the sides of the box. In addition, a clear acetate window cover was placed over the box bottom. A gold foil sticker naming the fashion was affixed to the acetate cover — printing on the stickers has been found in red or black. Dolls were sewn into their box (correct box bottom will have two holes from stitches) with no box liner included.

### NRFB $295.00+ each

# SKIPPER

Skipper doll dressed in #1901 Red Sensation; right – Skipper doll dressed in #1902 Silk 'n Fancy. Notice the typographical error on Red Sensation reads "Rensation."

Backs of dressed boxed dolls shows threads where dolls were sewn into boxes. Red or black nylon thread was taped to box bottom and acetate cover.

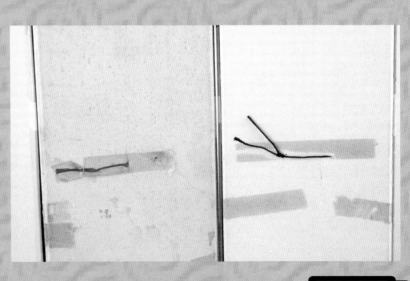

# SKIPPER

*Left – 1966 bend-leg doll with pink skin tone; right – 1965 bend-leg doll with tan skin tone.*

### 1030 – Bend-Leg Skipper (1965)

This year Skipper doll had new, bendable legs. In appearance, this doll is similar to the straight leg doll. Her differences are bendable legs, a new swimsuit, and a brand new box. Skipper doll's available hair colors remained the same. This year the hair color was printed on the box or on a white sticker and attached to the box end flap. The box is dated 1964 and her accessories included a "gold" wire stand, booklet, white comb and brush, brass headband, and swimsuit.

> Markings:
> ©1963
> Mattel, INC

### NRFB $195.00+; M/C $95.00+

### 1030 – Bend-Leg Skipper (1966)

In 1966 Mattel introduced a new pink skin tone which was used for Skipper doll and her friends. Skipper dolls and friends from this year are found in both the regular tan skin tone and the newer pink skin. The new, pink skin tone is often referred to by collectors as the "Mod" skin tone, and was used on all dolls beginning in 1967. The box, dates, markings and accessories remained the same as the 1965 bend-leg Skipper doll.

### NRFB $195.00+; M/C $95.00+

### 1030 – Bend-Leg Skipper (1967)

This doll was identical to the previous bend-leg Skipper dolls, with the exception of a very rare box style and packaging. The preceding bend-leg box was in two pieces, with Skipper doll's photo on the box lid. For 1967 the box lid was essentially turned over (so Skipper doll's photo was on the back) and a new liner inserted inside the lid. The sides of the box, now in lime green, depicted mod era fashions. The Skipper doll logo was now in teal (instead of rose), and Skipper doll's photo remained the same. The entire box was cellophaned, with an adhesive yellow identification sticker placed in the lower front. As with the 1966 bend-leg Skipper doll, this doll was also available in either the tan or the pink skin tone. Stock number and markings remained the same.

### NRFB $425.00+

*Collection of Cynthia Chapman*

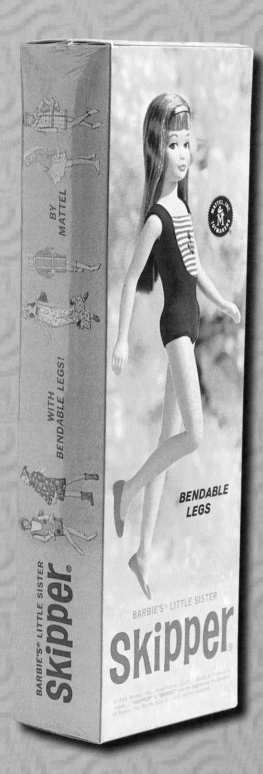

BENDABLE
LEGS

BARBIE'S® LITTLE SISTER
**Skipper**®

Collection of Sandi Holder

BY MATTEL

*Third outfit from the right was not produced.*

### 1105 – Twist 'n Turn Skipper (1968)

This year Skipper doll got a new look! She had a new swimsuit, rooted eyelashes, cheek blush, and new lip color. She also got a new Twist 'N Turn (TNT) waist, and a new box with mod graphics (however the box still bears the 1963 copyright stamp). Hair colors available were ash and pale blonde, titian, and brunette. Many of the dolls are found with vibrant cheek blush and beautiful pale skin. Her accessories included a white comb and brush, black eyelash comb, new clear plastic "X" stand (which doubled as a seat when turned over), turquoise elastic headband, swimsuit, and booklet. The first part of the year dolls were made in Japan (and marked Japan), then late in the year the dolls were produced in Taiwan (and marked Taiwan).

> Markings:
> ©1967 Mattel, Inc.
> U.S. Pat'd.
> U.S. Pats. Pend.
> Made in Japan – or –
> Made in Taiwan

**NRFB $295.00+; M/C $85.00; $125.00+ for high color dolls**

Box end flap shows hair color sticker and stock number.

Hair colors available on the 1968 TNT blondes are the hardest to find. Swimsuit second from right is a rare variation in a textured, striped fabric.

### 1105 – Twist 'n Turn Skipper (1969)

In 1969 Skipper doll updated her straight hairstyle with two shoulder length sausage curls, held in place with bright orange bows. This doll was available with either Gold Blonde or Java Brown hair color. She wore a new orange and pink checked swimsuit and her accessories included a white comb and brush, black eyelash comb, clear plastic "X" stand, and booklet.

Markings:
©1967 Mattel, Inc.
U.S. Pat'd
U.S. Pats. Pend
Made in Taiwan

**NRFB $295.00+; M/C $150.00+**

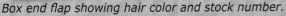

*Box end flap showing hair color and stock number.*

BY MATTEL

### 1105 – Twist 'n Turn Dressed Box Skipper (1969)

This doll, dressed in #1968 Hopscotchins, has the skinny wrist tag found on dolls used in store displays. Because this doll was purchased from a former Mattel employee, it is generally agreed that she was sent back to Mattel by a vendor (or never used), repackaged, and sold at the Mattel company store which was open to employees only.

### NRFB $395.00+

# SKIPPER

### 1105 – Twist 'n Turn Skipper (1970 – 1971)

The 1970 TNT Skipper doll was identical to the 1969 issue, with the exception of a new box and swimsuit. She was also available in either Gold Blonde or Java Brown hair color. Her accessories included a white comb and brush, black eyelash comb, clear plastic "X" stand, and booklet.

> Markings:
> ©1967 Mattel, Inc.
> U.S. Pat'd
> U.S. Pats. Pend
> Made in Taiwan

**NRFB $295.00+; M/C $125.00+**

*Box end flap shows hair color and stock number.*

*Note the difference in the box artwork between the original straight-leg Skipper doll (on right) and the reissue Skipper doll (on left), including an updated Mattel logo.*

## 0950 – Reissue Skipper (1970 – 1971)

The original 1964 straight–leg Skipper doll reappeared on the scene this year with the new, pink skin tone. She had all the same characteristics and accessories as the original doll of 1964, including her stock number. However, her gold wire stand was replaced with the new clear plastic "X" stand. At first glance her box appears to be the same as the 1964 box, but upon closer inspection, you will notice new artwork depicting fashions from the early '70s Skipper doll line. On the front of the box PJ doll has replaced Midge doll, and Barbie doll wears her TNT swimsuit and new flip hairstyle. Today these dolls are often found with lips that have faded to light pink or yellow, the arms have faded, and the faces often have green spots. This doll is very hard to find especially with original, unfaded coral lips. She was available in blonde, brunette, and redhead.

> Markings:
> ©1963
> MATTEL, INC.

## NRFB $425.00+; M/C $75.00+

*Barbie doll's new friend PJ doll has replaced her best friend Midge doll on the reissue box front.*

# SKIPPER

## 1147 – Living Skipper (1970)

This year an articulated, living Skipper doll was introduced featuring a new body style with swivel waist, hips, neck, wrists, and shoulders, and bendable elbows and knees. In addition to a new body, Skipper doll also got a new hairstyle available in either strawberry blonde or pale blonde, and a new swimsuit. Her accessories included a clear plastic stand (now called a "free posin'" stand) and booklet. Her Trade-In Special box is dated 1970. This doll could be purchased for $1.99 with the trade-in of a played with Mattel family doll.

Markings:
©1969 MATTEL INC TAIWAN
U.S. & FOR. PATD
OTHER PATS.PEND.
PATD IN CANADA 1967

**NRFB $125.00+; M/C $45.00+**

## 1117 – Dramatic New Living Skipper (1970)

This doll is identical to the Living Skipper right down to the swimsuit. The difference in these dolls is their name (Living Skipper is used only on the Trade-In Special box), stock number, and box style (box is dated 1969).

Markings:
©1969 MATTEL INC TAIWAN
U.S. & FOR. PATD
OTHER PATS.PEND.
PATD IN CANADA 1967

**NRFB $125.00+; M/C $45.00+**

*Left – strawberry blonde; right – pale blonde, which is VHTF.*

# SKIPPER

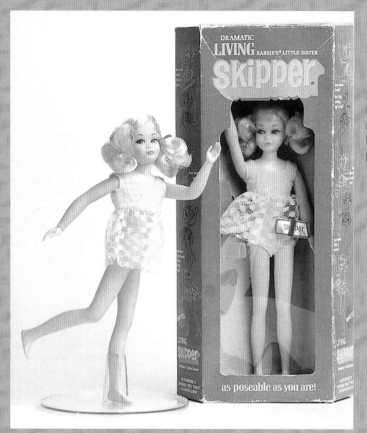

### 1117 – Dramatic Living Skipper (1971)
Essentially the same as the 1970 issue, the 1971 Dramatic Living Skipper doll had a new box style (dated 1970) a new yellow swimsuit, and new accessories. Her accessories included an orange skateboard, a brand new two-piece clear plastic stand, and booklet. This packaging is VHTF.

> Markings:
> ©1969 MATTEL INC TAIWAN
> U.S. & FOR. PATD
> OTHER PATS.PEND.
> PATD IN CANADA 1967

**NRFB $325.00+; M/C $85.00+**

*This doll's swimsuit is VHTF. This new, clear stand was used for the Live Action Barbie doll line.*

## 1069 – The Sun Set Malibu Skipper (1971 – 1974)

The Sun Set Malibu Skipper doll reverted back to her old, straight hairstyle but changed in many other ways. Skipper doll now had "sun-tanned" skin, a two-piece orange tricot swimsuit, new face paint, and a new bubble box style (dated 1970). Package is trimmed in either copper or lavender. Her accessories included a blue terrycloth towel and lavender sunglasses. NRFB dolls have been found with and without wrist tags.

Markings:
©1967
Mattel, Inc.
U.S. Pat'd.
U.S. Pats. Pend.
Made in Japan

**NRFB $95.00+; M/C $25.00+**

# SKIPPER

### 1179 – Pose 'n Play Skipper (1972 – 1973)
Sold with the Swing-A-Rounder Gym gift set. See Chapter 6, page 204, for photo and description.

### 1117 – Pose 'n Play Skipper – Baggie (1973)
In 1973 Mattel sold dolls in a clear plastic bag with a cardboard header. Introduced as a method of clearing out old Mattel stock, they are referred to by collectors as "baggie" dolls. Her package is dated 1973 with a copyright date of 1967, and is available in either strawberry blonde or the HTF pale blonde.

> Markings:
> ©1969 MATTEL. INC.
> TAIWAN
> U.S. & FOR PATD
> OTHER PATS PEND
> PATD IN CANADA 1967

**NRFB $125.00; M/C $35.00+**

*Pale blonde hair color of doll on right is VHTF.*

## 4223 – Quick Curl Skipper (1973 – 1975)

This doll had the addition of metal fibers in her hair to allow the hair to be curled and to stay in place. Her accessories included a pink comb and brush, plastic hair curling wand, yellow and blue hair ribbons, two white metal barrettes, white Taiwan flats, and fashion booklet. Two different box styles were produced.

Markings:
©1967 Mattel Inc.
Taiwan
U.S. Patented.
Other Patents Pending

**Left: Common Box – NRFB $95.00+; M/C $35.00+**
**Right: HTF Box – NRFB $125.00+; M/C $15.00+**

Chapter 1

### 7259 – Growing Up Skipper (1975 – 1977)

This new body style was unusual because it was "2 dolls in 1 for twice as much fun!" When Skipper doll's left arm was rotated forward, she grew taller and developed small breasts, making her "grow from a young girl to a teenager in seconds!" She was dressed in a red body suit with a blue removable collar and a red and white houndstooth checked skirt. Her accessories included red flats, white platform sandals, a long red and white houndstooth checked skirt, a blue tricot scarf, red hairband, red tricot socks, and booklet. She came in either strawberry blonde or pale blonde.

Markings:
©1967
MATTEL INC.
HONG KONG
U.S. & FOR. PAT

**NRFB $75.00+
(both box styles)
M/C – $35.00+**

*Directions show how to make Skipper doll grow up.*

*A red headband hidden in Skipper doll's long hair is often missing on loose dolls.*

# SKIPPER

### 7379 – Gold Medal Skipper (1975 – 1976)

"Our U.S. Olympic Favorite!" Malibu Skipper doll, authorized by the U.S. Olympic Committee, wears a red, white, and blue one-piece suit, and a "gold" medal. This doll came in an unusual solid cardboard box that did not allow the purchaser to see the doll inside.

| Markings: |
| :---: |
| ©1967 Mattel Inc. |
| U.S. Pat'd |
| U.S. Pats Pend |
| Made in Korea |

**NRFB $85.00+; M/C $30.00 – 40.00**

### 7379 – Simpatia Skipper (1977)

An Italian-issued counterpart to the Gold Medal Malibu Skipper doll, this doll wears a one-piece suit of yellow, orange, and turquoise tricot. She has an unusual square-shaped Mattel wrist tag in white with blue printing. The box is the same solid cardboard style as the U.S. version, with different graphics.

| Markings: |
| :---: |
| ©1967 Mattel Inc. |
| U.S. Pat'd |
| U.S. Pats Pend |
| Made in Korea |

**NRFB $80.00+; M/C $30.00 – 40.00**

### 1069 – The Sun Set Malibu Skipper (1975)

Identical to the 1974 issue, this doll came in a new white window box design.

| Markings: |
| :---: |
| ©1967 |
| Mattel, Inc. |
| U.S. Pat'd. |
| U.S. Pats. Pend. |
| Made in Korea |

**NRFB $95.00+; M/C $25.00+**

# SKIPPER

### 9428 – Deluxe Quick Curl Skipper
### (1976 – 1977)

This doll was packaged in a new box style, beginning what collectors now to refer to as the "Pink Box" era. Skipper doll's unusual hair fiber was the same as the 1973 issue, which allowed the hair to be instantly curled without heat or water. She wore a pink maxi dress with shirred bodice, lace-trimmed sleeves, a white crocheted shawl, and a white plastic bead necklace. Her accessories included a white plastic comb, brush, curling wand, blonde fall that tied on to her hair with pink ribbon, two white metal barrettes, yellow and blue hair ribbons, and pink shoes.

Markings:
©1967 Mattel Inc.
U.S. Pat'd.
Made in Taiwan

**NRFB $95.00+; M/C $30.00+**

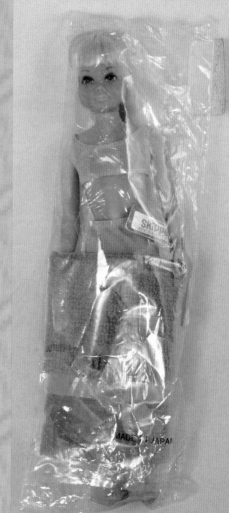

### 1069 – "Baggie" Sears Malibu Skipper
### (1978 – 1979)
An unusual Skipper doll sold without a box.
**NRFB: $35.00+**

# SKIPPER

*Loose doll on right is the 1978 Malibu from the first part of the year. The center doll is from the latter part of 1978. Notice the lighter makeup.*

## 1069 – Malibu Skipper (1976 – 1977)

This doll, identical to the previous edition Sun Set Skipper, came packaged in the new "pink box" style. Canadian Malibu Skipper dolls sold in 1977 had the same yellow, orange, and turquoise swimsuit as the Italian #7379 Simpatia doll.

| Markings: |
| --- |
| ©1967/Mattel, Inc. |
| U.S. Pat'd. |
| U.S. Pats. Pend. |
| Made in Korea |

**NRFB $75.00+; M/C $20.00+**

## 1069 – Malibu Skipper (1978 – 1979)

A slight change to the box size and graphics was the only noticeable difference to Malibu Skipper doll this year. During the first part of the year, the doll was made in Korea. During the latter part of the year the doll was made in the Philippines, and has a smaller head and less eye makeup.

| Markings: |
| --- |
| ©1967 |
| Mattel, Inc. |
| U.S. Pat'd. |
| U.S. Pats. Pend. |
| Made in Korea |
| – OR – |
| ©Mattel, Inc. |
| 1967/Philippines |

**NRFB $60.00+; M/C $20.00+**

## 1069 – Malibu Skipper (1978 – 1979)

The Italian #7379 Simpatia Skipper doll swimsuit boxed for U.S. market.

**NRFB: $50.00+**

# SKIPPER

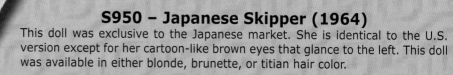

## S950 – Japanese Skipper (1964)

This doll was exclusive to the Japanese market. She is identical to the U.S. version except for her cartoon-like brown eyes that glance to the left. This doll was available in either blonde, brunette, or titian hair color.

Markings:
©1963
MATTEL, INC.

### NRFB $500.00+; M/C $275.00+

*A close-up view of the hair colors.*

# SKIPPER

## Japanese Dressed Box Skipper Dolls (1964 – 1965)

A 1964 standard Japanese Skipper doll was available in dressed boxed versions. These differ from the U.S. market dolls in the following ways: the Japanese market doll included a round black stand with Skipper in gold lettering; the box lids did not have white bands; the stock number was a paper label attached to the bottom of the box lid which corresponds to the outfit stock number; there were no holes in the box bottoms where the dolls were sewn in for the U.S. market; some (and possibly all) Japanese dolls included a postage stamp-sized tarrif sticker inside the top corner of the box bottom. Also included with the doll was a Japanese market booklet that shows all of the available fashions dressed on Japanese Skipper dolls with the round black stands. We believe all of these were available as dressed boxed dolls.

### NRFB: $1,000.00+

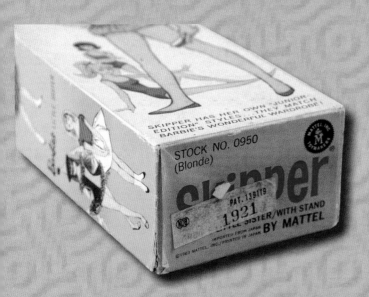

# SKIPPER

S 1918
¥ 700

S 1919
¥ 700

S 1920
¥ 700

S 1921
¥ 700

S 1922
¥ 700

S 2001
¥ 700

S 1910
¥ 700

S 1911
¥ 700

S 1912
¥ 700

S 1913
¥ 700

S 1914
¥ 700

S 1915
¥ 700

S 1916
¥ 700

S 1917
¥ 700

S 1901
¥ 700

S 1902
¥ 700

S 1904
¥ 700

S 1905
¥ 700

S 1906
¥ 700

S 1907
¥ 700

S 1908
¥ 700

S 1909
¥ 700

## 1069 – Sun Set Skipper – Japan (1972)

Probably the most beautiful of all vintage Skipper dolls is this version of the Malibu Skipper, available only in Japan. Incredibly rare, this doll has brown eyes, rooted eyelashes, cheek blush, soft pink lips, and luscious, long brunette hair. Her swimsuit, towel, and markings are identical to the U.S. version.

**NRFB $1,500.00+; M/C $750.00+**

# SKIPPER

### 8519 – Twist 'n Turn Skipper – Europe (1972 – 1973)

This doll was not available for sale in the United States. Her hair and facial features are similar in style to the 1964 straight-leg Skipper doll. However, she came with a TNT waist, straight legs, pink skin tone, and was available in either blonde (uncommon) or dark brunette hair color. Her swimsuit fabric and style are unique to this doll.

Markings:
©1967 Mattel Inc.
U.S. Pat'd
U.S. Pats. Pend
Made in Taiwan

**NRFB $650.00+; M/C $150.00+**

### 8126 – Twist 'n Turn Skipper – Europe (1974)

With TNT waist and bendable knees, this doll was available for only one year. She wore a two-piece navy tricot swimsuit.

Markings:
©1967 Mattel
U.S. Pat'd
U.S. Pats. Pend
Made in Korea

**NRFB $125.00; M/C $35.00+**

### 7193 – Funtime Skipper – Europe (1974)

This doll came packaged in a white window-styled box similar to the U.S. version Sun Set Malibu Skipper. The doll has pale pink skin, coral lips, vivid eye makeup, pale blonde hair, and a yellow tricot two-piece swimsuit.

Markings:
©1967 Mattel Inc.
U.S. Pat'd
U.S. Pats. Pend
Made in Korea
(marked Korea at waistline)

**NRFB $75.00+; M/C $15.00+**

# SKIPPER

## 9926 – Partytime Skipper – Europe (1976 – 1979)

Dressed in a yellow satin party dress with lace and ribbon trim, Skipper doll has pale blonde hair and a very pink skin tone. The doll has a TNT waist and unusual soft vinyl legs that do not bend.

Markings:
©MATTEL Inc.
1967
Philippines

**NRFB $50.00+; M/C $25.00+**

Collection of Carol Spencer

## 8126 – Best Buy Dressed Boxed Doll

Barbie dolls dressed in Best Buy-era outfits and packaged on blister cards were sold in Australia and possibly other foreign markets during the 1970s. This Skipper doll is the only example we have been able to find dressed and in this kind of packaging. It is possible that this is a sample doll, but if it were actually sold at retail, additional NRFB examples may be wearing other outfits.

**NRFB $125.00+**

### Skip-Chan – Japan (1976)

Skip-Chan is a dressed box doll that was available wearing four different outfits, none of which were sold separately. Box indicates dolls were manufactured in Japan and the Philippines. The dolls included a pair of hard plastic flats (without country of origin stamped) and a fashion booklet. Left to right: S1301 – white satin party dress with pink trim; S1201 – hot pink satin dress with yellow flower accent; S1202 – floral top with gold "suede" collar and pink cotton skirt. Not pictured (see catalog illustration at right) is S1302, a coral party dress with a white waist bow. S1301 and S1302 cost 100 yen more than S1201 and S1202.

### NRFB $150.00+; M/C $35.00+

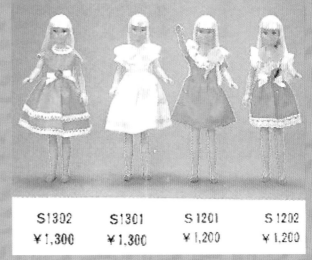

| S1302 | S1301 | S1201 | S1202 |
|---|---|---|---|
| ¥1,300 | ¥1,300 | ¥1,200 | ¥1,200 |

## European Market Spin-Around Store Display Sign (1966 – 1967?)

An unusual and incredibly rare store display sign, this three-sided metal sign features Skipper, Skooter, Barbie, Midge, Ken, and Allan dolls. Printed in French, Dutch, and English, it features the Mattel S.A. International logo and is manufactured by ebiex. This is the type of item that thrills collectors and makes collecting vintage items so fun. The sign was never available for purchase and was meant to be thrown out after the promotion was over, so the fact that this one still exists is amazing! These items are difficult to assign a value to, and are often sold at a price the buyer feels comfortable with. Sign is 14" tall; with base, about 18".

# Chapter 2
# The Friends

# The Friends

Skipper doll's world rapidly expanded with the introduction of two new friends in 1965, Skooter doll and Ricky doll. They were the same size as Skipper doll, so the child (or parent) did not have to buy different clothes to include the new doll in their play patterns. Since then, Mattel has created many new Skipper friends, always Skipper-sized. Because the friends are manufactured in smaller quantities than Skipper, they can be more difficult to find.

## 1040 – Straight-Leg Skooter (1965 – 1967)

Skooter doll made her debut in 1965 as Skipper's friend. She was initially produced with a tan body, solid vinyl legs, brown eyes, freckles, and two pigtails held in place with deep red bows. Eventually her tan body was replaced with the new pink skin tone in 1966. Her hair colors are the basic brunette, titian, and pale blonde, and are so marked on her box end flap. Her accessories included a two-piece red and white swimsuit, "Skooter" wrist tag, booklet, gold metal stand, red flats, comb, and brush.

> Markings:
> ©1963
> Mattel, Inc.

**NRFB $175.00+; M/C $75.00+**

*The three hair colors of Skooter doll with tan skin tone on left and pink skin tones on right.*

# The Friends

## 1120 – Bend-Leg Skooter
## (1966 – 1967)

"With 'Lifelike' Bendable Legs," Skooter doll had a new box and swimsuit consisting of blue jean shorts and red and white polka dot ruffled top (a rare variation was also made in orange with white polka dots). She was initially produced in the tan skin tone, and later changed to the new pink tone. The hair colors, markings, and accessories remained the same as the Straight-Leg Skooter from 1965.

Markings:
©1963
Mattel, Inc.

**NRFB $275.00+**
**M/C $85.00+ (tan skin)**
**$95.00+ (pink skin)**

*Three tan skin-toned dolls on left and three pink tones on right.*

# The Friends

## 1090 – Ricky (1965 – 1967)

Another one of Skipper doll's friends introduced in 1965 was Ricky. He had the same body and markings as the 1964 Skipper doll, which meant he could technically wear all of Skipper's fashions; but why would he do that when he could have his own wardrobe? In addition to Ricky doll, six new Ricky doll fashions were also introduced. It's interesting to note that of all Skipper doll's friends, Ricky was the only one to have his own, tagged ensembles. In 1965 he was produced in the tan skin tone, then in 1966 he was sold in the new pink skin tone. He has painted red hair, blue eyes, and freckles. His accessories included blue shorts, multicolored striped jacket, red and cork sandals, "Ricky" wrist tag, liner, booklet, and black metal stand.

> Markings:
> ©1963
> Mattel, Inc.

### NRFB $175.00+; M/C $65.00+

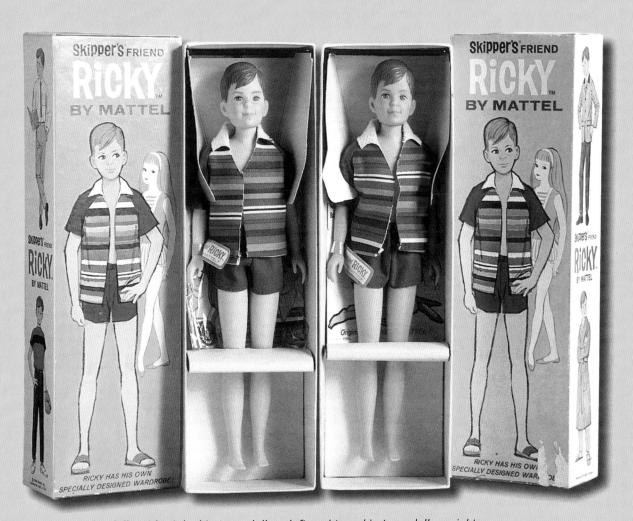

*NRFB Ricky dolls with pink skin tone doll on left and tan skin tone doll on right.*

# The Friends

## Ricky Fashions

### 1501 – Lights Out (1965 – 1967)

This set includes yellow cotton two-piece pajamas with white collar, pocket trim, and three white buttons; light blue terrycloth robe with matching belt; and light blue terrycloth scuffs.

**Variation:** Robe was also produced in a dark blue terrycloth with matching scuffs.

### NRFB $65.00+; M/C $40.00 – 45.00

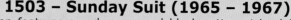

### 1502 – Saturday Show (1965 – 1967)

This ensemble contains tan cotton slacks with zipper and button closure; white cotton long-sleeved shirt with breast pocket and three buttons; red cotton tie (shorter than Ken doll's); red cotton knit socks; and black tennis shoes.

### NRFB $65.00+; M/C $40.00 – 45.00

### 1503 – Sunday Suit (1965 – 1967)

This fashion features a red, gray, and black cotton striped jacket with black collar, two mock pockets, and three black buttons; white cotton short-sleeved shirt with three buttons; black cotton slacks with zipper and button closure; red cotton knit socks; and black tennis shoes.

### NRFB $65.00+; M/C $40.00 – 45.00

# The Friends

## 1504 – Little Leaguer (1965 – 1967)

This set comes with a red cotton knit short-sleeved shirt with navy blue stripe; blue denim jeans with zipper; brown vinyl baseball glove; red vinyl baseball cap with a white painted "M"; white plastic baseball; red cotton knit socks with navy blue stripe at the top; and white tennis shoes.

### NRFB $75.00; M/C $40.00+

## 1505 – Skateboard Set (1965 – 1967)

This ensemble features a white cotton short-sleeved shirt with red and gray pin stripes and four red buttons; white cotton shorts with zippered front; white cotton knit socks; beige plastic skateboard with painted red stripe; and white tennis shoes.

**Variation:** Shirt was also produced in fabric from Ricky's #1503 Sunday Suit.

### NRFB $75.00+; M/C $40.00+

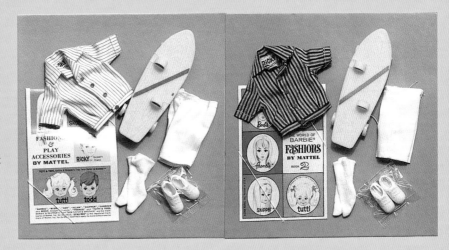

## 1506 – Let's Explore! (1965 – 1967)

This group has a red plaid long-sleeved flannel shirt with three black buttons; gray or black cotton slacks with zipper and button closure; red cotton knit socks; and black tennis shoes.

**Variation:** Shirt was also produced in fabric from Ken's #1409 Going Huntin'.

### NRFB $95.00; M/C $60.00+

# The Friends

## 1199 – Pose 'n Play Tiff (1972)

Tiff was introduced this year as "Skipper's Tomboy Friend!" She has medium length, titian, center–parted straight hair, brown eyes with painted eyelashes, and body construction the same as Pose 'n Play Skipper. She was made with the Dramatic New Living Fluff head mold. Her accessories included white velour sleeveless top with a "Stop" decal on front, blue jeans with red "Help!" and "Go!" decals on each pant-leg, "Tiff" wrist tag, white tennis shoes with red painted trim, and a red plastic skateboard. This doll is VHTF.

Markings:
©1969 Mattel, Inc.
Taiwan
U.S. & For. Patd.
Other Pats. Pend.
Patd. In Canada 1967.

### NRFB $395.00+; M/C $200.00+

## 1143 – Dramatic New Living Fluff (1971)

Dramatic New Living Fluff was introduced this year as Dramatic Living Skipper's playmate. She has brown eyes, rooted eyelashes, and blonde hair styled into two pigtails held in place with orange hairbows. Her body was the same construction as her counterpart Dramatic Living Skipper. Her accessories included a one-piece play suit with yellow, orange, and green striped knit bodice, solid orange vinyl skirt with two yellow buttons and attached shorts, yellow plastic skateboard, "Fluff" wrist tag, and a round, clear plastic "real posin' stand."

Markings:
©1969 Mattel, Inc.
Taiwan/U.S. & For. Patd.
Other Pats. Pend.
Patd. In Canada 1967

### NRFB $175.00+; M/C $85.00+

*Prototype Mattel heads; left – Tiff with variation hairstyle and glued-on eyelashes; right – Living Skipper with very pale blonde hair and unusual pale pink hair ribbons.*

# The Friends

## 521-16038 – Chocho Chan/Butterfly Skipper – Japan (1974 – 1975)

Chocho means butterfly in Japanese, and this doll is often referred to as Butterfly Skipper. The box packaging does not refer to Chocho as a friend of Barbie or Skipper doll; however, the doll has the Deluxe Quick Curl Skipper body. The doll came with quick curl hair in blonde, brunette, or titian pigtails tied with orange ribbon. She wore a full-length red or hot pink satin dress with pink ribbon trim and a yellow felt butterfly appliqué. Her accessories included yellow cardboard butterfly wings (to be worn as a hair ornament by a child), pink quick curl comb, brush and curler, yellow and green hair ribbons, two white metal barrettes, and orange flats. This doll is VHTF.

> Markings:
> ©1967 Mattel Inc.
> Taiwan U.S. Patented
> Other Patents Pending.

### NRFB $175.00+; M/C $95.00+

## Chocho Chan Outfits

Fashions marketed for Chocho Chan were identical to Skipper doll's outfits sold in the U.S., but with different stock numbers and packaging. Pictured here (left to right) are 522-79999, 522-79975, and 522-79968. The back of the blister pack shows other 1974 Best Buy outfits available in the U.S.

### NRFB $40.00+

## 9222 – Growing Up Ginger (1976)

Growing Up Ginger was made from the same head mold and had the same body construction as Growing Up Skipper. She has long brunette, straight, side-parted hair, and brown eyes with painted eyelashes. Her accessories included a turquoise body suit with pink velvet attached collar and three white buttons, two cotton turquoise and white polka dotted skirts (one long and one short), pink tricot neck scarf and ankle socks, turquoise flats, and white platform sandals.

> Markings:
> ©1967
> Mattel, Inc.
> Hong Kong
> U.S. & For. Pat
> Patented Canada
> 1974

**NRFB $95.00+; M/C $45.00+**

# The Friends

### 7381 – Funtime Skooter – Europe
### (1976 – 1977)

This extremely HTF Skooter doll was available exclusively throughout Europe and is the most difficult doll to find of all Skipper doll's friends. She has very beautiful deep auburn hair that is styled in a flip, turquoise blue eyes with painted eyelashes, soft orange lips, and heavy cheek blush. This doll was produced using the Skipper head mold, and has a TNT waist and bendable knees. She is dressed in a two-piece turquoise tricot bathing suit. This doll is RARE.

Markings:
©1967 Mattel, Inc.
U.S. Pat'd.
U.S. Pats Pend/Made in Korea

**NRFB $195.00+; M/C $125.00+**

Collection of Kitty Stuart

# The Friends

Mattel's Barbie doll family was one of the hottest toys sold in the 1960s. Many manufacturers sought to imitate the product and profit from the growing fashion doll market by producing a less expensive and usually inferior product. Skipper doll had a number of competitors, some of them close copies and others that are hideously ugly. These dolls don't have the same, solid feeling as Skipper because they're made of lightweight plastic, their skin colors run from bright pink to dark gray, they have oddly jointed limbs and/or necks, and their facial paint is often "out of focus."

Companies that produced these knock-off or clone dolls sometimes sold matching ensembles for them that were often direct copies of Mattel manufactured clothing. Some are very well made and often appear to be authentic, but these clothing pieces are usually not lined or finished to Mattel's standards, and do not have "Skipper" clothing tags.

The clone dolls are quite inexpensive and can provide hours of amusement. The graphics on the original packages are great, but NRFB examples are difficult to locate. These dolls and their clothes present a three-dimensional look at what can be produced when profit, instead of a quality toy that children can play with and enjoy for years, is a company's highest priority.

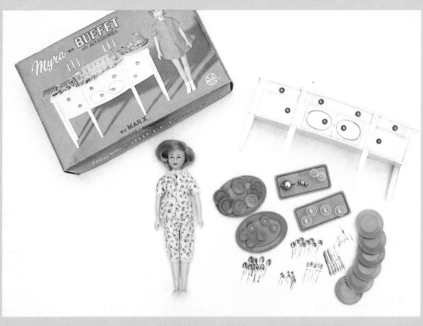

Collection of Barb Mitchell

## Myra with Buffet and Accessories by Marx

This is an elaborate and well-made set. Myra's older sister Marlene came with a vanity and was a competitor to Barbie doll.

*Values on these items vary widely due to personal interest in collecting them.

## Miss Gwen

This doll looks as if her face mold were taken directly from Skipper doll's. The face is made of a very strange, squishy vinyl, and the box is marked "British Colony of Hong Kong."

# The Friends

## Miss Kitty by Cragstan

This is an adorable, freckle-faced doll whose swimsuit and clothing ensembles are direct knock-offs of Skipper doll's.

Collection of Barb Mitchell

## Miss Teen Hatbox Case

This case features a Skipper-like doll wearing Town Togs. The case is printed "Miss Teen," a registered trademark, 1966.

Collection of Barb Mitchell

*The names and manufacturers of the three loose dolls are unknown. Miss Pre-Teen, by Princess Grace Doll Company, may have been manufactured by the same company that produced Miss Gwen. The NRFB Sandy outfit by Elite Creations has some great accessories.*

51

# The Friends

Collection of Barb Mitchell

Collection of Barb Mitchell

## Peggy by Plasty

This beautifully made, German doll's accessories included a stand that matched her shoe color. The assortment of NRFB outfits shows the range of clothing available for this doll, from mild mid-'60s to way-out '70s.

The backs of Peggy's clothing boxes show the different Peggy dolls through the years. The blonde doll used on the lower left packaging is actually a Francie doll knock-off named Lorraine.

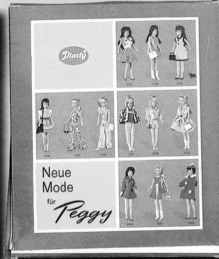
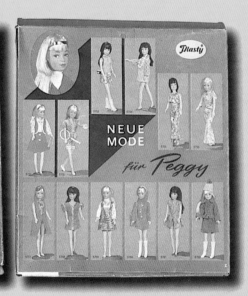

# Chapter 3
# Skipper Doll's World of Fashion

# Skipper Doll's World of Fashion

The wardrobe! The concept behind the selling point of the original dolls is very different from that of today. The child usually had only one doll and maybe a friend doll, and new clothing ensembles were purchased to spark the child's imagination during playtime. Today, dolls are dressed with a theme for play, so every new play idea has a different doll associated with it.

Skipper doll's wardrobe included pieces for school, play, special occasions, and formal events. The clothing reflects the innocence of the era as well as the idea that a young girl was actually a young lady and needed to have matching hats, handbags, hose and gloves for her outfits. Mattel designers were encouraged to include as many accessories as they could in the early outfits such as tiny spoons, yo-yos, balls, and phonograph records. Safety regulations and cost reduction have forced many of these items to be omitted from toys today.

## A Key to Terms Used in This Section

We have used the following terms to describe certain items:

**Pantyhose** – made of sheer nylon, the two legs are sewn together.
**Stockings** – thigh-high single stockings of sheer, opaque, knit, lace, or patterned fabric.
**Tights** – opaque tricot, lace, or knit fabric, with the two legs sewn together.
**Ankle boots, rain boots,** and **knee boots** are all made of soft, squishy vinyl. Hard plastic boots are from knock-off doll ensembles.
**Japan flats** – first issue Skipper doll shoes, used until mod era (some overlap).
**Taiwan flats** – larger than Japan flats to accommodate bend-leg doll feet, wider color range.
**Squishy Taiwan flats** – generally came with outfits that had pantyhose, stockings, or tights.

## Skipper Fashion Tray (1965 – 1966)

This VHTF countertop display tray was available only to retailers. Items like this are highly sought after by collectors because they were usually thrown away after the sales promotion ended or to make way for new stock.

### $100.00+ (outfits not included)

# Skipper Doll's World of Fashion

## 1900 – Underpretties (1964 – 1965)

Set includes a white dotted sheer nylon petticoat; white tricot panties; light pink plastic mirror, comb, brush, and four hair rollers.

**NRFB: $95.00+; M/C: $15.00 – 25.00**

## 1901 – Red Sensation (1964 – 1965)

Set includes a red cotton dress with rickrack trim and four silver or gold buttons; white straw hat with red ribbon hatband and streamers; short white tricot gloves; white tricot socks; and red Japan flats.

**NRFB: $95.00+; M/C: $35.00 – 45.00**

 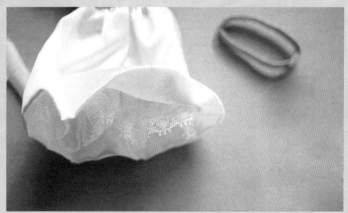

## 1902 – Silk 'n Fancy (1964 – 1965)

Set includes a dress with red velvet bodice, gold braid waistband, and white satin skirt with a ruffled underskirt in either white or red and white lace; gold elastic headband; white tricot socks; and black Japan flats.

### NRFB: $95.00+; M/C: $40.00 – 55.00

# Skipper Doll's World of Fashion

## 1903 – Masquerade (1964 – 1965)
Set includes a black and yellow cotton mini-dress with black and yellow tulle trim; black cotton panties; black and yellow felt hat with chinstrap; black plastic mask with black elastic band; yellow paper invitation; and black Japan flats with yellow pompons.

### NRFB: $100.00+; M/C: $60.00 – 75.00

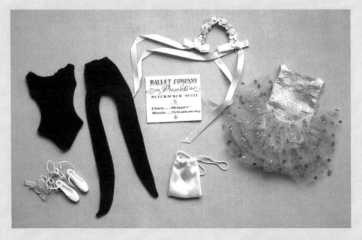

## 1904 – Flower Girl (1964 – 1965)
Set includes a pale yellow cotton dress with lace overskirt and yellow bow at waist; yellow headpiece of velvet flowers and yellow ribbon streamers; small bouquet of flowers with yellow and white ribbon streamers and lace base; short white tricot gloves; white tricot socks; and white Japan flats.

### NRFB: $100.00+; M/C: $40.00 – 55.00

## 1905 – Ballet Class or Ballet Lessons (1964 – 1965)
Set includes a pink lamé tutu with ruffled pink tulle skirt; black leotard; black tights; pink satin ballet slipper bag with drawstrings; white vinyl ballet slippers; floral headpiece with pink streamers; and white paper program.

### NRFB: $100.00+; M/C: $50.00 – 65.00

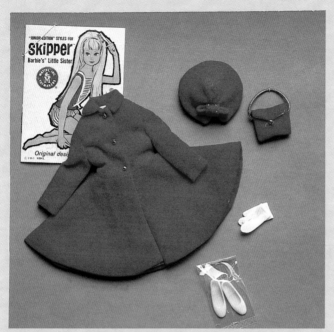

## 1906 – Dress Coat (1964 – 1965)

Set includes a red velvet full-skirted coat with three gold bead accents; red velvet purse with gold cord handle and gold bead closure; red velvet hat with attached matching red bow; short white tricot gloves; and white Japan flats.

### NRFB: $75.00+; M/C: $35.00 – 50.00

## 1907 – School Days (1964 – 1966)

Set includes a pink knit cardigan sweater with four gold bead closures; white short-sleeved cotton blouse with two white plastic buttons; pink flannel pleated skirt with snap closure in back; wooden bowl with three balls of yarn and two knitting needles; pink or white tricot knee-high socks; and squishy black Japan flats.

### NRFB: $100.00+; M/C: $40.00 – 55.00

## S2001 – Skipper Kimono – Japan
## (1964 – ?)

This set includes a formal kimono of white brocade with red and gold pattern; red and gold brocade obi (waist sash); clutch purse that matches kimono fabric or drawstring bag that matches obi fabric; pair of pokkuri (high Japanese sandals) or zori (sandals) and tabi (socks).
*This outfit is VERY RARE.*

### M/C: $1,500.00+

Collection Keiko Shibano

## 1908 – Skating Fun
## (1964 – 1966)

This is a full-length body suit made of nylon knit containing a white turtleneck on top and red tights on bottom; red velvet skirt lined in red calico print with matching shoulder straps; white fur hat with red calico ties and lining, and a red pompon (pompon usually fades to orange); white fur muff with red calico lining; and white vinyl ice skates with gray plastic blades.

### NRFB: $95.00+
### M/C: $40.00 – 50.00

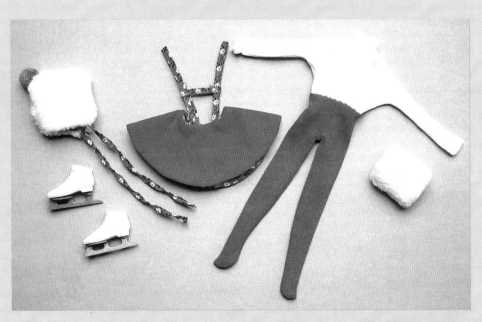

59

### 1909 – Dreamtime (1964 – 1966)

This ensemble features white with pink polka dot cotton pajamas trimmed in white lace; pale pink flannel robe with dark pink ties, and a kitten appliquéd on pocket; light blue princess phone; red paper phone directory; blue felt stuffed cat; and dark pink felt scuffs with light pink fringe.

**NRFB: $95.00+; M/C: $35.00 – 45.00**

### 1910 – Sunny Pastels (1965 – 1966)

This fashion ensemble contains a cotton sleeveless shift dress in pastel-colored horizontal stripes, pink tree print with six gold sequin accents; matching purse with dark pink tree print and three gold sequin accents; white tricot socks; and pink Japan flats.

**NRFB: $95.00+; M/C: $35.00 – 45.00**

## 1911 – Day at the Fair (1965 – 1966)

This set includes a "Barbie" printed sleeveless cotton body suit in red, blue, green, and white with two white plastic buttons; matching head scarf; red cotton wrap-around skirt with red plastic belt, gold buckle closure, and Barbie print pocket; miniature "Barbie" doll to fit in pocket; and red Japan flats.

### NRFB: $175.00+; M/C: $95.00 – 115.00

**Variation:** The skirt was produced in rare dark pink cotton.

61

### 1912 – Cookie Time (1965 – 1966)

This ensemble features a cotton dropped-waist dress with sleeveless bodice in white with five red buttons, skirt in navy blue with white stitching, and red braid belt with metal buckle; metal bowl; metal spoon with red handle; wood rolling pin with red handles; cardboard box of "Cookie Mix" mix; cardboard *Barbie Easy as Pie* cookbook; and red Japan flats.

**NRFB: $125.00+; M/C: $55.00 – 65.00**

### 1913 – Me 'n My Doll (1965 – 1966)

This fashion ensemble contains a pink gingham cotton sleeveless dress with three red rose appliqués on a white front bodice and pink grosgrain ribbon shoulder straps; pink tricot petticoat with lace trim; miniature "Barbie" doll; tiny pink gingham skirt for the miniature "Barbie" doll; white tricot socks; and white Japan flats.

**NRFB: $140.00+; M/C: $110.00 – 150.00**

**Variation:** Petticoat with lace trim was also produced in the same trim as Barbie doll's Pak Lingerie.

# Skipper Doll's World of Fashion

### 1914 – Platter Party (1965)

This ensemble features a full-length dress with blue velvet bodice and white organdy collar, skirt of red, blue, and green plaid trimmed with red ball fringe; blue plastic record player; two records with blue and red "Barbie" doll labels; and red Japan flats.

**NRFB: $125.00+; M/C: $50.00 – 60.00**

### 1915 – Outdoor Casuals (1965 – 1966)

This set includes a pair of turquoise Capri pants; turquoise knit dickey (HTF); turquoise cable knit sweater with large roll collar; red wooden yo-yo; short white tricot gloves; and white Japan flats.

**NRFB: $125.00+; M/C: $40.00 – 60.00**

### 1916 – Rain or Shine (1965 – 1966)

This fashion ensemble contains a yellow cotton raincoat with matching belt with gold buckle; yellow cotton rain hat with bill; yellow umbrella with white plastic handle and yellow tassel; and white knee-high boots.

**NRFB: $75.00+**
**M/C: $25.00 – 40.00**

## 1917 – Land and Sea (1965 – 1966)

This set includes a pair of light blue denim pedal pusher pants with red stitching; light blue denim pullover middy jacket with red drawstrings and stitching; light blue denim gob cap with red stitching; red and white horizontal striped knit short-sleeved top; red plastic sunglasses (same design as sunglasses from Barbie doll's #941 Tennis Anyone); and white Japan flats.

### NRFB: $125.00+; M/C: $50.00 – 65.00

## 1918 – Ship Ahoy (1965 – 1966)

This ensemble features a dropped-waist, long-sleeved dress with pleated skirt; red, white, and blue striped knit bodice with navy blue cotton skirt; navy blue cotton sailor-collared vest with six gold bead accents; red plastic toy sailboat with a white plastic sail; black plastic camera; Hawaii and Mexico paper travel brochures; white tricot socks; and red Japan flats.

### NRFB: $150.00+; M/C: $75.00 – 95.00

# Skipper Doll's World of Fashion

## 1919 – Happy Birthday (1965)

The sleeveless cotton party dress in this set has a light blue bodice with lace front and blue ribbon tie at neck, blue ribbon sash, and a white skirt with blue floral embroidery. Other items include a white cotton petticoat with blue embroidery; white straw hat with light blue hatband; optional light blue satin hair ribbon (VERY RARE); gold wrapped present with white ribbon, pink felt flower, and red tag; white plastic cake with brown or yellow icing; six pink plastic candles with red tips; round white paper doily with scalloped edge; white paper invitation with dark pink text; two pink party favors; two napkins; short white tricot gloves; white tricot socks; and white Japan flats.

**NRFB: $250.00+; M/C: $195.00 – 225.00**

## 1920 – Fun Time (1965 – 1966)
This set includes dark blue cotton Capri pants; dark blue cotton jacket with three green toggle-look accents and pocket trim; dark blue cotton sleeveless top with an embroidered floral design on front; blue, green, and brown plaid short-sleeved cotton blouse with two green plastic buttons (same fabric as Ken doll's #1416 College Student); wooden croquet mallet; wooden croquet stake; wooden croquet ball; two wire wickets; and royal blue Japan flats.

**NRFB: $150.00+**
**M/C: $65.00 – 80.00**

## 1921 – School Girl (1965 – 1966)

This set comes with a red cotton blazer with school insignia on pocket and two gold bead buttons; red checked pleated cotton skirt (same as Barbie doll's #1622 Student Teacher); white sleeveless cotton blouse with red stitching and two red buttons; three school books: yellow "English," blue "Geography," and green "Arithmetic"; two wooden pencils (dark brown and red); black vinyl book strap; dark brown glasses with clear plastic lenses (VHTF); red felt hat with band of red checked fabric (same as skirt) and white feather; red and yellow wax apple; white tricot socks; and red Japan flats.

**NRFB: $200.00+; M/C: $125.00 – 150.00**

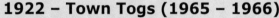

### 1922 – Town Togs (1965 – 1966)

This set includes a green felt jumper with two pleats, yellow stitching, and two gold bead accents; green felt jacket with three gold bead buttons and matching belt with gold buckle; yellow knit turtleneck; black and white checked thigh-high stockings and matching cap with bill; and black Japan flats.

### NRFB: $125.00+; M/C: $60.00 – 75.00

# Skipper Doll's World of Fashion

### 1923 – Can You Play? (1966)

This ensemble features blue shift dress with red polka dots and red and white polka dot ruffle trim; red scarf with white polka dots; red panties with white polka dots; red and white jump rope; white plastic ball (larger than the ball found in Barbie doll's #941 Tennis Anyone); and red Japan flats.

### NRFB: $95.00+; M/C: $35.00 – 45.00

### 1924 – Tea Party (1966)

This set includes yellow shift dress with flocked white flowers and ruffled hem (flocking is almost always worn off); silver teapot and lid with "B" monogram; two plastic turquoise teacups and saucers; two silver spoons; two white placemats with yellow and turquoise stitching; two Styrofoam pieces of cake with pink frosting; one plastic turquoise plate; and yellow Japan flats.

### NRFB: $175.00+; M/C: $125.00 – 150.00

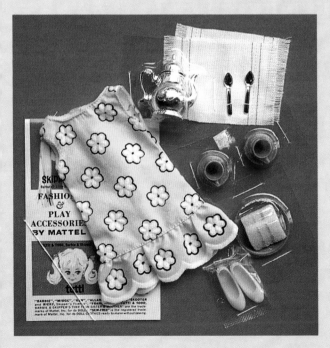

*Note how odd it is that only one plate was sold in this set when all other accessories are in pairs.*

## 1925 – What's New at the Zoo? (1966)
This set contains a red cotton dropped-waist dress with white braid trim placket and three red plastic buttons; white cardigan sweater with red trim; and red Japan flats.
**Warning:** Red trim in sweater bleeds when laundered.
**NRFB: $95.00+; M/C: $35.00 – 40.00**

## 1926 – Chill Chasers (1966)
This set comes with a white fur coat with four red buttons; red felt tam hat with navy pompon; white tricot socks (not shown); and red Japan flats.
**Variation:** Jacket was also produced with white buttons.
**NRFB: $75.00+; M/C: $40.00 – 50.00**

## 1928 – Rainy Day Checkers (1966)

This fashion ensemble features a red and blue plaid long-sleeved dress with white lace collar; red felt vest with four gold beads; red tricot thigh-high stockings; red and black cardboard checkerboard; plastic checkers, 12 red and 12 black (VHTF); and black Japan flats.

**NRFB: $225.00+; M/C: $150.00 – 175.00**

## 1929 – Dog Show (1966)

The set comes with a dark pink cotton short skirt with two red pleats; white cotton sleeveless top with pink knit trim, Scottie dog silk-screened on front; white dog with blue felt eyes, black bead pupils, pink felt tongue, black felt nose, and white felt ears (VHTF); red braid leash; cardboard box of dog food; and red Japan flats.

**NRFB: $150.00+**
**M/C: $125.00 – 150.00**

## 1930 – Loungin' Lovelies (1966)

This set includes aqua tricot pajamas with white lace trim; aqua quilted robe with lace cuffs and collar, lace-trimmed pocket, and white ribbon waistband; and aqua felt scuffs with white lace trim.
*The felt scuffs are VHTF.

**NRFB: $95.00+; M/C: $45.00 – 65.00**

Chapter 3

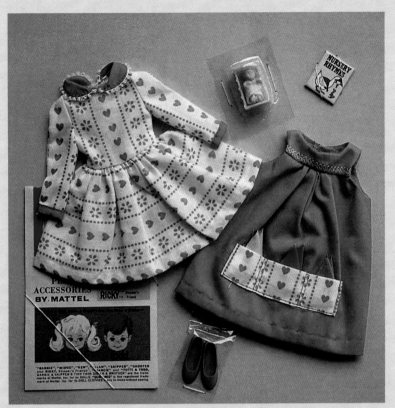

### 1932 – Let's Play House (1966)
This set includes a white and turquoise heart and flower print long-sleeved dress; turquoise pinafore with three pockets from dress fabric; three handkerchiefs in yellow, pink, and green cotton; plastic baby doll with a glued-on white diaper; pink and blue plastic cradle; cardboard *Nursery Rhymes* book (VHTF); and turquoise or light blue Japan flats.

**NRFB: $175.00+**
**M/C: $110.00 – 125.00**

## 1933 – Country Picnic (1966)
This set comes with a pink, green, and blue cotton sleeveless dress with three butterflies appliquéd on skirt; matching cotton bag; red checked blanket with red fringe; red checked napkin; four-color rubber beach ball in blue, red, green, and yellow; red plastic Thermos with blue top, or blue Thermos with red top, and Scottie dog decal on front; plastic ice cream cone with cotton ice cream; plastic hamburger; plastic drinking glass with pink "liquid"; plastic hot dog on metal BBQ fork with red handle; plastic blue plate with or without embossed pattern; wax watermelon slice; paper Monarch butterfly; butterfly net; and pink Japan flats
*This outfit is VHTF complete with the butterfly and handle on Thermos cap.*

**NRFB: $395.00+**
**M/C: $295.00+**

## 1934 – Junior Bridesmaid (1966)

This set comes with a pink taffeta full-length dress with lace net overlay; pink tulle hat with pink flowers around face pink plastic basket of blue and pink flowers with pink satin bow accent; long white organdy petticoat with tulle trim and tie at waist; white tricot socks; short white tricot gloves; and white or pink Japan flats.

*This outfit is VHTF in mint condition.*

### NRFB: $300.00+
### M/C: $200.00 – 250.00

### 1935 – Learning to Ride (1966)

This set includes a black and white checked riding jacket with three black plastic buttons; red sleeveless knit top; yellow cotton jodhpurs with vinyl patches; black plastic riding hat; black plastic riding crop (HTF); black plastic knee-high boots; and short black tricot gloves (HTF).

**NRFB: $175.00+; M/C: $125.00+**

### 1936 – Sledding Fun (1966)

This ensemble features blue knit pants with red knit stocking feet sewn in; red and white calico quilted jacket with zipper front and white faux-fur collar; red cotton knit sleeveless top; blue hood with matching calico ties; white fur and red knit mittens; red plastic sled with white runners and string; and red galoshes.
*This outfit is HTF.*

**NRFB: $195.00+**
**M/C: $125.00 – 150.00**

## 1938 – Beachy Peachy (1967)

This set includes a yellow floral two-piece swimsuit with yellow rickrack trim; yellow floral cover-up dress with yellow rickrack trim; yellow metal headband (VHTF); pink plastic bag with white fabric flower accent; and yellow Japan flats.

**Variation:** The cover-up was also produced in the fabric from #1924 Tea Party, and the swimsuit was produced without the pink printed flower centers.

### NRFB: $125.00+; M/C: $65.00 – 80.00

Photo courtesy of Marcie Melillo

### 1939 – Flower Showers (1967)
This ensemble features a blue floral vinyl raincoat with zipper; matching hood with gold bead closure; blue and pink plastic belt with gold metal buckle; and hot pink galoshes.

**NRFB: $95.00+**
**M/C: $45.00 – 60.00**

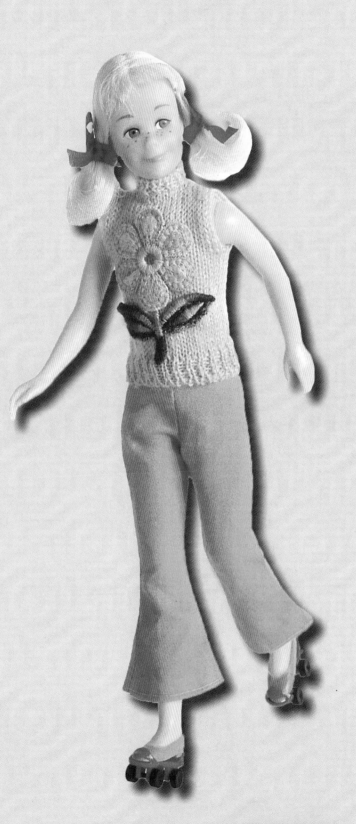

### 1940 – Rolla Scoot (1967)

This fashion ensemble contains orange cotton bell-bottom pants; pink sleeveless sweater with flower appliqué on front; pink Japan flats; and plastic red rollerskates with clear loop straps (VHTF) and black wheels.

**NRFB: $150.00+**
**M/C: $95.00 – 110.00**

# Skipper Doll's World of Fashion

### 1941 – All Spruced Up (1967)

This set includes a black and white tweed dress with white collar, red grosgrain ribbon ties, and five black plastic buttons (same fabric as Barbie doll's #954 Career Girl); white hat with red grosgrain ribbon trim; white plastic shoulder bag with red stitching; white lace thigh-high stockings; and black Japan flats.

**Variation:** Dress was also produced in the fabric from Ken doll's #1424 Business Appointment.

*Red ribbons on the dress and hat have nearly always faded to orange.*

**NRFB: $150.00+**
**M/C: $75.00 – 95.00**

### 1943 – Popover (1967)

This set comes with a long-sleeved white lace dress with ruffled hem and cuffs; white lace thigh-high stockings; white lace hood with button closure (HTF); hot pink vinyl jumper lined in green vinyl with three circular cutouts to show the green lining, and three applied yellow vinyl dots (produced in either glossy or matte finish); and white Japan flats.

*The jumper's vinyl has hardened to an extremely brittle state, making it impossible to dress on a doll.

**NRFB: $150.00+; M/C: $60.00 – 75.00**

## 1942 – Right in Style (1967)

This set comes with a green and white floral cotton short-sleeved dress with green waistband; green cotton jumper with two pockets and white stitching; green and white floral cotton hat; black plastic granny glasses (HTF); white tricot socks; and green Japan flats.

**Variation:** This fashion was also produced in a turquoise version with a turquoise jumper, turquoise waistband on dress, and turquoise flats, and is VHTF.

**NRFB: $150.00+; M/C: $85.00 – 110.00**

## 1944 – Jamas 'n Jaunties (1967)

This set includes a white sleeveless jumpsuit in orange, fuchsia, and green floral pattern with lace and ribbon trim; matching mob cap; white shorts in orange and fuchsia floral pattern with lace trim; matching slip; white floral lace pantyhose (exclusive to this fashion); four pink plastic hair rollers; and bright pink felt scuffs.

**NRFB: $150.00+**
**M/C: $75.00 – 90.00**

### 1945 – Hearts 'n Flowers (1967)

This set includes a blazer in lime green, floral and heart pattern with four yellow buttons; matching jumper-style dress with two silver buckles and attached yellow ribbed tank top; matching cap; yellow vinyl shoulder bag with vinyl shoulder strap; yellow ribbed knit knee-high socks; two books, green "Arithmetic" and yellow "English"; two wooden pencils, tan and red; black vinyl book strap; black granny glasses (VHTF); and yellow ankle boots.

**Variation:** Fashion also produced in a VHTF pale blue, pink, and green floral print

**Green Version:**
**NRFB: $150.00+**
**M/C: $95.00 – 125.00**

**Blue Variation:**
**NRFB: $350.00+**
**M/C: $175.00 – 200.00**

### 1946 – Glad Plaids (1967)

This set contains a white, yellow, and fuchsia plaid coat with six fuchsia plastic buttons; matching plaid skirt; matching plaid purse with gold chain strap and pearl button closure; fuchsia knit sleeveless top; fuchsia and yellow vinyl belt with gold metal buckle; fuchsia knit cap with vinyl visor; light yellow lace, thigh-high stockings (VHTF); and white ankle boots (VHTF).

*This outfit is VHTF.*

**NRFB: $125.00+**
**M/C: $80.00 – 95.00**

## skipper®

## 1947 – Lolapaloozas (1967)

This set contains a bright pink cotton sleeveless crop top with green floral print and ruffled hem; bright pink and green polka dot cotton bell-bottom pants; bright pink cotton shorts with green floral print; bright pink cotton sleeveless top with elastic waistband in green polka dots and stripes; bright pink and green polka dot cotton jacket with green ruffled short sleeves; green cotton short skirt with bright pink and green striped pleat and dotted belt with buckle; and hot pink squishy Taiwan flats.

### NRFB: $125.00+; M/C: $80.00 – 95.00

## 1948 – Velvet 'n Lace (1967)

This set includes a long-sleeved red velvet dress with white lace bodice; red velvet coat with faux fur collar and cuffs; white tricot gloves; white tricot socks; and black squishy Japan or black shoes with silver buckles. These are Francie doll's squishy buckle flats with foil buckles glued on (RARE).

### NRFB: $150.00+
### M/C: $80.00 – 95.00

# Skipper Doll's World of Fashion

## 1949 – All Prettied Up (1967)

This set contains a dark pink long-sleeved drop-waist dress with lace overskirt and lace cuffs; white lace thigh-high stockings; and white Japan flats.

**Variations:** This fashion was also produced in pale pink chiffon, or with overskirt in white embroidered organdy.

### NRFB: $100.00+; M/C: $60.00 – 75.00

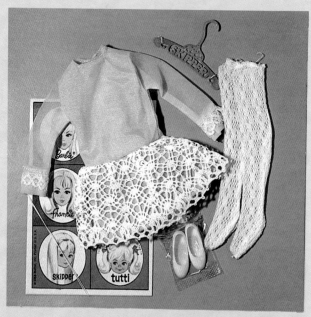

# Skipper Doll's World of Fashion

## 1955 – Posy Party (1968)

This set includes a blue floral cotton dress with center pleat and long sleeves, empire waist, trimmed with hot pink ribbon band and bow, sleeves trimmed in lace; hot pink taffeta petti-pants with matching floral ruffle trim; plastic hot fudge sundae; metal spoon (HTF); white lace thigh-high stockings; and hot pink squishy Taiwan flats.
**Variation:** This fashion was also produced in a lighter blue floral print.

### NRFB: $150.00+; M/C: $60.00 – 75.00

## 1956 – Skimmy Stripes (1968)

This ensemble contains a bright orange knit long-sleeved dress with multicolored stripes; matching knit socks; bright orange felt cap with (or without) attached plastic lime green granny glasses; two books, green "Arithmetic" and yellow "English"; two pencils, wooden tan and red; black vinyl book strap; and orange ankle boots.

### NRFB: $150.00+
### M/C: $95.00 – 110.00

# Skipper Doll's World of Fashion

### 1957 – Baby Dolls (1968)

This outfit includes a pink nylon shortie pajamas with white lace trim, blue braid, and hot pink bow; pink plastic comb and brush (not shown); and hot pink felt scuffs with blue braid trim.

**NRFB: $75.00+**
**M/C: $35.00 – 50.00**

### 1958 – Patent 'n Pants (1968)

This emsemble contains a cotton pantsuit with denim pants and white sleeveless top with blue and red polka dots; red vinyl belt with gold buckle; red vinyl double-breasted coat with six gold bead buttons, white braid sleeve trim, and polka dot lining; and red Japan flats.
Note: The pantsuit is the same design as the Skipper doll Pak, Summer Slacks; see Chapter 5.

**NRFB: $100.00+; M/C: $45.00 – 60.00**

## 1959 – Warm 'n Wonderful (1968)

This fashion set includes a blue and green striped knit dress with drop-waist; blue and green color-blocked fuzzy coat with green vinyl trim; blue vinyl cap (same design as #1935 Learning to Ride); green fishnet thigh-high stockings (HTF); and blue vinyl knee-high boots.

### NRFB: $125.00+
### M/C: $55.00 – 70.00

## 1960 – Trim Twosome (1968)

This emsemble contains a sleeveless white, orange, pink, and beige striped cotton pleated dress with three gold bead buttons on bodice; white crinkle polyester coat with four gold bead buttons and white satin lining; white and hot coral striped vinyl belt with gold buckle; neon orange vinyl purse with gold bead closure; and translucent neon orange Taiwan flats.
*This outfit is VHTF.*

### NRFB: $100.00+
### M/C: $50.00 – 65.00

### 1961 – Real Sporty! (1968)

This fasion set showcases a yellow cotton romper with hot pink stitching; matching yellow cotton jacket with four pink buttons; hot pink plastic "chain" belt (VHTF); hot pink lace tights; and hot pink ankle boots.

*This outfit does not come with the pink felt cowboy hat with which it is shown in the fashion booklets.*

**NRFB: $135.00+**
**M/C: $45.00 – 60.00**

Chapter 3

# Skipper Doll's World of Fashion

### 1962 – Quick Changes! (1968)

This ensemble contains a light blue sleeveless shift dress with orange front zipper; light blue and orange pleated cotton skirt; light blue, pink, and orange knit sweater with four gold bead buttons; pink knit knee-high socks with orange tassels; and hot pink ankle boots.

**NRFB: $100.00+**
**M/C: $45.00 – 60.00**

### Confetti Cutie (Sears Exclusive) (1968)

This set includes a yellow cotton jumper with center pleat; turquoise and yellow knit long-sleeved turtleneck; matching socks; gold chain belt; turquoise vinyl hat (same design as #1935 Learning to Ride); and yellow ankle boots.
*This outfit is RARE.*

**NRFB: $495.00+**
**M/C: $250.00+**

Collection of Cheryl Nelson

## 1966 – Jeepers Creepers
## (1969 – 1970)

This set includes an orange top with blue polka dots (printed fabric or silk-screened dots); blue shoulder straps and hem trim; orange and blue striped cotton pedal pusher pants; orange plastic sun visor with blue cotton ties with orange plastic cinch ring; blue and orange rubber ball (VERY RARE); and light blue Taiwan flats.

### NRFB: $150.00+
### M/C: $75.00 – 95.00

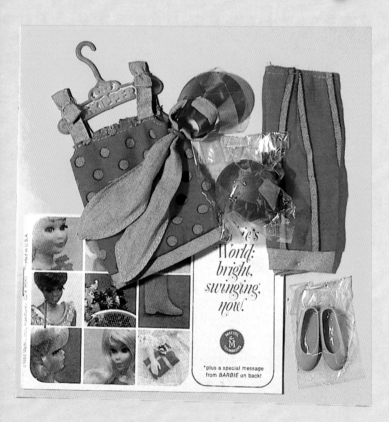

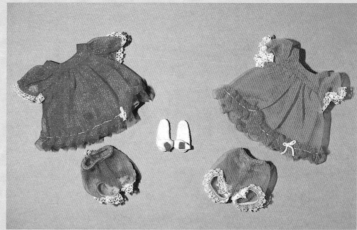

### 1967 – Jazzy Jamys (1969 – 1970)

This set has sheer, deep coral nylon pajamas with orange nylon lining, white lace sleeve trim, and white nylon bow at hem; and white felt scuffs with matching coral nylon trim.

**NRFB: $75.00+; M/C: $35.00 – 45.00**

### 1968 – Hopscotchins (1969 – 1970)

This ensemble contains a long-sleeved cotton shirt with pink, green, yellow, and blue stripes and three gold bead buttons; green cotton shorts with two pockets and yellow vinyl belt loops; pink and yellow striped plastic belt with gold buckle; and blue Taiwan flats.

**NRFB: $95.00+; M/C: $35.00 – 50.00**

# Skipper Doll's World of Fashion

## 1969 – Knit Bit (1969 – 1970)

This set includes a hot pink knitted sleeveless dress with rickrack trim and two blue buttons; blue knit belt; hot pink tricot shorts; blue knitted headband with hot pink rickrack accent; plastic hot fudge sundae (optional); red and white jump rope (optional); hot pink tricot knee-high socks; and hot pink ankle boots.

**NRFB: $100.00+**
**M/C: $50.00 – 75.00**

## 1970 – Ice Cream 'n Cake (1969 – 1970)

This ensemble contains a white cotton long-sleeved blouse with white lace trim and three blue buttons; turquoise cotton, pleated skirt; turquoise under-shorts with white lace trim (HTF); pink vinyl belt with gold buckle; white lace thigh-high stockings; and white Taiwan squishy flats.

**NRFB: $100.00+; M/C: $60.00 – 75.00**

# Skipper Doll's World of Fashion

### 1971 – Pants 'n Pinafore (1969 – 1970)

This set incudes an orange cotton romper with yellow vinyl "belt" and two gold bead buttons; white ruffled apron (different fabrics available); orange cotton head scarf with ruffle; and orange translucent Taiwan flats.

### NRFB: $95.00+; M/C: $45.00 – 60.00

### 1972 – Drizzle Sizzle (1969 – 1970)

This fashion ensemble contains a pink and green (olive or kelly) knit dress with orange vinyl appliqué flowers; clear vinyl raincoat with orange trim; clear vinyl rain hat with orange trim; and clear vinyl rain boots with orange trim.

### NRFB: $125.00+; M/C: $50.00 – 65.00

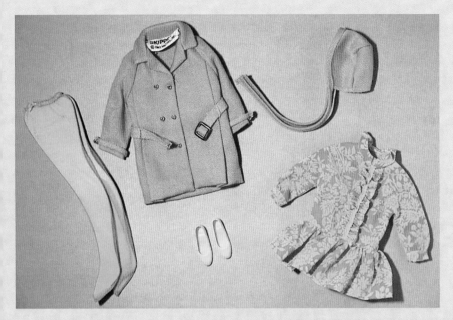

## 1973 – Chilly Chums (1969 – 1970)

Chilly Chums includes a pink cotton, drop-waist dress with yellow floral print and ruffled placket; pink cotton double-breasted coat with six gold bead buttons; pink cotton belt with gold buckle; pink cotton hood with ties; sheer pink nylon pantyhose; and yellow squishy Taiwan flats (HTF).

### NRFB: $100.00+
### M/C: $60.00 – 75.00

## 1974 – Eeny Meeny Midi
## (1969 – 1970)

This set contains a yellow cotton dress with lace overlay, ruffled hem, and yellow ribbon at waist; yellow tricot petti-pants with lace trim; orange wrapped present with yellow ribbon and white flower accent; white cardboard mirror with face on back; and yellow Taiwan flats.

**Variation:** The dress came in purple paisley cotton with white lace overlay and no ribbon trim. Tagged, but most likely a Mattel sample.

### NRFB: $100.00+
### M/C: $40.00 – 60.00

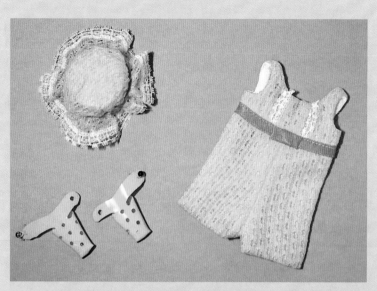

### 1975 – Sunny Suity (1969 – 1970)

This outfit has a yellow cotton, princess-waist romper with white lace bodice trim and hot pink ribbon belt; matching yellow lace sun hat with hot pink elastic band; and yellow vinyl sandals with holes and gold bead buttons.

**NRFB: $75.00+**
**M/C: $40.00 – 55.00**

### 1976 – School's Cool (1969 – 1970)

This ensemble includes a green and pink cotton floral print dress with white dotted Swiss collar and short sleeves (print on dress varies); hot pink fishnet or opaque orange tights; pink, rose, or hot pink princess telephone (optional); and hot pink ankle boots.

**NRFB: $95.00+**
**M/C: $45.00 – 60.00**

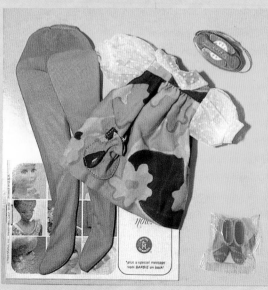

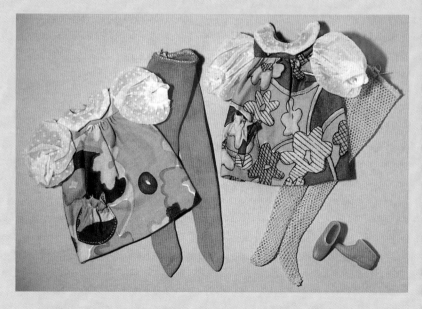

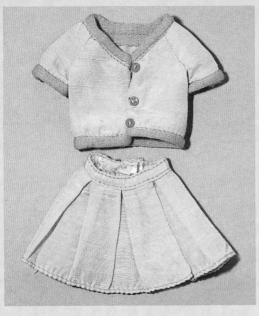

## 1977 – Plaid City (1969 – 1970)

This set features a lime green polished cotton pleated skirt; lime green polished cotton jacket with blue trim and three blue buttons; blue knit wrap-around dickey with blue button (VHTF); white, blue, and lime green plaid coat with blue knit collar and seven blue buttons; blue knit tam with pompon; and lime green translucent Taiwan flats (HTF).

**Variation:** Skirt and jacket can also be found in lime green raw silk.

*This outfit is HTF.*

### NRFB: $125.00+; M/C: $75.00 – 90.00

# Skipper Doll's World of Fashion

### 1730 – Lots of Lace (1970)

This set contains a long-sleeved, kelly green turtleneck dress with multi-layered white lace skirt and yellow ribbon "belt"; and lime green translucent Taiwan flats (HTF).

**NRFB: $75.00+; M/C: $20.00 – 30.00**

### 1731 – Budding Beauty (1970)

This fashion ensemble features a hot pink organdy dress with long sleeves, lined skirt, white taffeta bodice with pale pink flocked flowers, and lime green ribbon at waist; and hot pink squishy Taiwan flats.

**Variations:** Dress of pale pink organdy with matching lining and bodice of pale pink lace, or hot pink organdy dress with bodice of white cotton with rose print from Francie doll's #3369 Pink 'n Pretty.

**NRFB: $75.00+; M/C: $25.00 – 35.00**

Collection of Priscilla Wardlow

# Skipper Doll's World of Fashion

## 1732 – Daisy Crazy (1970)

This set features a hot pink knit dress with yellow tricot daisy print sleeves, collar, and attached belt; yellow tricot daisy-print (HTF) or hot pink tricot knee-high socks; and yellow Taiwan flats.

### NRFB: $75.00+
### M/C: $30.00 – 45.00

## 1733 – Rik Rak Rah (1970)

This ensemble contains a blue cotton playsuit with white and yellow rickrack trim and white elastic waistband; white cotton skirt with yellow and blue rickrack trim, yellow vinyl suspenders, and two yellow buttons; and blue Taiwan flats.

**Variation:** The skirt was also produced in fabric from #1932 Let's Play House.

### NRFB: $75.00+
### M/C: $25.00 – 35.00

Collection of Priscilla Wardlow

## 1736 – Super Slacks (1970 – 1971)

This set has a white blouse with white lace placket; red bell-bottom pants with white floral print and red vinyl shoulder straps with two white buttons; matching red with white floral print hat with red vinyl bill; red sunglasses; and red Taiwan flats.

**NRFB: $95.00+; M/C: $35.00 – 50.00**

## 1735 – Twice as Nice (1970 – 1971)

This fashion set includes a blue and pink felt coat with two fake pockets and one gold bead button; blue and pink felt dress; pink felt hat with pompon; and blue Taiwan flats.

**Variation:** Orange and gold felt coat, orange and gold felt dress, gold felt hat with pompon, and orange Taiwan flats; VHTF.

**Blue – NRFB: $75.00**
**M/C: $35.00 – 45.00**

**Orange – NRFB: $150.00+**
**M/C: $60.00 – 75.00**

### 1737 – Velvet Blush (1970 – 1971)

This set features a red velour long-sleeved dress with white organdy collar and cuffs with white loop trim, and white organdy waistband with bow; white lace tights; and white Taiwan flats.

**NRFB: $95.00+**
**M/C: $35.00 – 50.00**

Variation, from the collection of Leslie Sena

## 1738 – Fancy Pants
## (1970 – 1971)

This set has a hot pink vinyl tank top with three tiers of light blue cotton floral ruffles; matching floral print pants with three ruffled tiers; light blue cotton shorts; hot pink vinyl bag with white button at handle and three yellow vinyl daisies with white button centers; and light blue Taiwan flats.

### NRFB: $95.00+
### M/C: $45.00 – 60.00

**Variation:** Top and pants also found in a horizontal material of orange, hot pink, and white stripes, and orange nylon shorts (VERY RARE).

## Variation
## NRFB: $400.00+; M/C: $200.00+

*Note that the ensemble came with HTF shorts.*

## 1746 – Wooly Winner (1970 – 1971)

This ensemble showcases a red wool coat with blue vinyl trim; matching red wool hat with blue vinyl trim; dress with red, blue, and yellow plaid skirt and yellow long-sleeved knit turtleneck; dark blue cotton knee-high socks; red vinyl shoulder bag; and dark blue ankle boots.

### NRFB: $95.00+; M/C: $50.00 – 65.00

## 1747 – Pink Princess (1970 – 1971)

This set contains a light green crinkle crepe coat with pink velvet ribbon trim and four gold bead buttons; pink sleeveless, crepe empire-waist dress with center pleat, three gold bead buttons and white lace trim; pink faux fur hat; hot pink sheer pantyhose, and white Taiwan flats.

### NRFB: $100.00+; M/C: $60.00 – 75.00

## 1748 – Triple Treat (1970 – 1971)

This set has a pair of turquoise velveteen pants with wide waistband of pink, green, and turquoise stripes (same fabric as Barbie's #1822 Swirly Cue); hot pink knit long-sleeved top; turquoise velveteen jacket with two pearl buttons; headscarf of pink, green, and turquoise striped material; dress with sleeveless bodice of striped material; turquoise velveteen skirt with lace trim at hem, pink velvet waistband, and attached pink flower; and turquoise Taiwan flats.

**Variation:** Swirly Cue fabric may be substituted with the multicolored material used in black Francie's swimsuit.

### NRFB: $125.00+; M/C: $50.00 – 65.00

## 1749 – Lemon Fluff (1970 – 1971)

This ensemble features a yellow fuzzy robe trimmed in yellow satin and yellow ribbon belt with fabric daisies on each end; yellow tricot pajamas with white lace trim; and yellow fuzzy scuffs.

### NRFB: $75.00+; M/C: $35.00 – 45.00

## 1513 – Young Ideas (Sears Exclusive) (1970 – 1973)

This set contains a plush coat with vinyl trim (this is the only tagged ensemble piece); party dress with rickrack edging and satin waistband with bow; two-piece suit: jacket and split skirt with vinyl waistband; knit sleeveless shell; knit kneesocks; two-piece playsuit: elastic waist shorts and sleeveless midi top with ruffle; sheer pantyhose; gold foil-wrapped present; "Come to my party" paper party invitation; red and white jump rope; green and yellow plastic ball (optional); and two pairs of Taiwan flats.

*This outfit recycled many fabrics used in other Barbie and related doll fashions. There are probably many more fabric variations yet to be discovered.

**NRFB: $195.00+**
**M/C: $75.00 – 125.00, depending on rare or unusual fabrics used**

*Knit socks and shell are always made from matching fabric.*

*A variety of previously used fabrics were recycled to create pieces for #1513 Young Ideas.*

## 3465 – Sweet Orange (1971 – 1972)
This set contains an orange velour full-skirted dress with drop-waist and white lace trim at cuffs, neck, hem, placket, and waistband with bow; and white Taiwan flats.

**NRFB: $75.00+; M/C: $20.00 – 25.00**

## 3466 – Tennis Time (1971 – 1972)
This ensemble includes a white cotton sleeveless tennis dress with pleated skirt and hot pink waist and neck trim; plastic tennis racket; plastic tennis ball; white tricot socks; and white tennis shoes or white Taiwan flats.

**NRFB: $75.00+; M/C: $25.00 – 40.00**

## 3467 – Teeter Timers (1971 – 1972)
This fashion set features a yellow cotton sleeveless top with pink floral pockets and stand-up collar; pink floral print pants; and yellow plastic teeter board with pink rails.
Note: This outfit does not come with yellow sandals or flats as it appears to in the Mattel dealer catalogs. The "sandals" are the straps on the teeter board.

**NRFB: $75.00+; M/C: $25.00 – 35.00**

### 3468 – Little Miss Midi (1971 – 1972)

This set includes a turquoise long-sleeved tricot blouse with three hot pink buttons or lime green tricot blouse (HTF); yellow cotton midi skirt with pink, blue, and green floral print; and turquoise vinyl knee-high boots.

**NRFB: $75.00+**

**M/C: $20.00 – 35.00**

### 3470 – Ice Skatin' (1971 – 1972)

This ensemble features an orange velour skating dress with three white buttons and white faux fur trim at hem; white faux fur hat with white ribbon ties; orange opaque tricot tights; and white vinyl ice skates with light gray plastic blades.

**NRFB: $75.00+**

**M/C: $20.00 – 35.00**

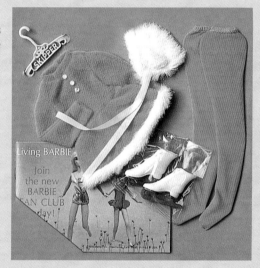

### 3471 – Ballerina (1971 – 1972)

This fashion set has a turquoise satin tutu with pink and turquoise tulle ruffled skirt and sleeves; sheer pink pantyhose; turquoise satin ballet bag with turquoise drawstring handles; and pale pink ballet slippers.

**NRFB: $75.00+**

**M/C: $35.00 – 50.00**

## 3472 – Double Dashers (1971 – 1972)

This set contains a navy knit coat with orange squares, orange collar, and two orange vinyl "frog" closures with four gold bead buttons; sleeveless orange cotton dress with navy trim and two gold bead buttons; and neon orange translucent Taiwan flats.

**NRFB: $75.00+; M/C: $25.00 – 35.00**

## 3473 – Lullaby Lime (1971 – 1972)

This ensemble includes a lime green tricot nightgown with lace shoulder straps, lime green sheer overlay with ruffled hem, and hot pink ribbon and bow at top of bodice; and hot pink felt scuffs with lime green tricot poufs (VHTF).

**NRFB: $65.00+**
**M/C: $25.00 – 35.00**

# Skipper Doll's World of Fashion

## 3475 – Goin' Sleddin' (1971 – 1972)

This ensemble includes a bright yellow faux fur, zip-front ski parka with hot pink trim; yellow floral sleeveless cotton top; hot pink pants; hot pink galoshes (HTF); and hot pink sled with yellow runners and string (HTF).

**NRFB: $125.00+; M/C: $75.00 – 95.00**

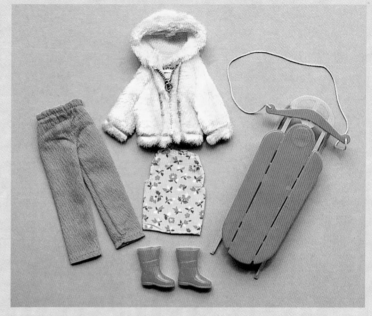

## 3476 – All Over Felt (1971 – 1972)

This set has a light blue and yellow felt sleeveless dress with two "pockets"; light blue felt coat with yellow felt placket and collar, stitched "pocket" detailing, one light blue felt "frog" closure and two gold buttons; light blue felt hat (VHTF); light blue sheer pantyhose (VHTF); yellow felt shoulder bag with yellow vinyl strap and gold bead button closure; and light blue Taiwan flats.

**Variation:** Light blue felt substituted with turquoise felt fabric.

**NRFB: $100.00+**
**(variation commands higher price)**
**M/C: $50.00 – 75.00**

### 3477 – Dressed in Velvet (1971 – 1972)

This ensemble includes a sleeveless dress with white bodice, pink velvet drop-waist skirt, lime green velvet ribbon waistband and bow with white braid trim and white braid trim at neck; pink velvet coat with oversized collar trimmed in white faux fur; matching faux fur-trimmed hat; pink sheer thigh-high stockings; and white Taiwan flats.

**NRFB: $125.00+**
**M/C: $60.00 – 80.00**

Chapter 3

## 3478 – Long 'n Short of It
## (1971 – 1972)

This fashion ensemble contains a sleeveless tricot mini dress of red with white and purple stripes at bodice or abstract print of red, white, and turquoise (same as Francie's #3449 Buckaroo Blues); matching long tricot scarf fringed in white; long red coat with three gold bead buttons and two "pockets" with gold bead buttons; white and red striped knit tam with red pompon; and red knee-high boots.

**NRFB: $95.00+**
**M/C: $50.00 – 65.00**

### 3291 – Nifty Knickers (1972)

This grouping features a long-sleeved yellow tricot shirt with elastic waist; sleeveless bib-style vest of red flock with side tabs, yellow contrast stitching, and two yellow buttons; blue floral knickers; and red knee-high boots.
*This outfit is HTF.*

**NRFB: $95.00+**
**M/C: $40.00 – 50.00**

# Skipper Doll's World of Fashion

### 3292 – Play Pants
### (1972)

This set contains denim short overalls with red stitching, red heart appliqué, and red vinyl straps with two gold bead buttons; white shirt with print design and red knit collar and cuffs; red knit kneesocks; and white tennis shoes.
*This outfit is HTF.*

**NRFB: $95.00+**
**M/C: $50.00 – 65.00**

### 3293 – Dream Ins
### (1972)

This ensemble showcases a pastel printed flannel nightgown with hot pink sheer ruffle trim at hem, sleeves, yoke, and tie at neck; and pink felt scuffs with sheer bows.
**Variation:** Nightgown also produced in white with yellow rosebud-print flannel material with yellow felt scuffs with sheer bows (HTF).

**NRFB: $50.00+**
**M/C: $20.00 – 35.00**

### 3295 – Turn Abouts (1972)

This set features a pair of red and yellow print knit pants; matching knit short skirt; matching knit tank top with yellow ribbed waistband; matching knit hat with red pompon; yellow ribbed shorts; long-sleeved shirt with yellow ribbed bodice and cuffs and red tricot sleeves; red plastic shoulder bag with yellow and red striped handle and tab closure; and red Taiwan flats.
*This outfit is HTF.*

**NRFB: $95.00+; M/C: $50.00 – 65.00**

### 3296 – Red, White 'n Blues (1972)

This ensemble contains a red, white, and blue heart-print maxi dress with red and blue ruffle trim at hem, yoke, and sleeves, and a blue tie belt; long-sleeved red tricot top, with blue and white braid V-neck and cuffs; blue cotton shorts with white braid trim; red tricot kneesocks; and blue Taiwan flats.
*This outfit is VHTF.*

**NRFB: $95.00+**
**M/C: $65.00 – 85.00**

**Variation:** Dress was made with multicolored print used in "Play Pants #3292.

### 3297 – Party Pair (1972)

This group has a pink velvet dress with white textured knit bodice insert and sleeves and floral braid trim; white faux fur coat with pink velvet collar, hem, and cuffs; pink sheer pantyhose; and pink Taiwan flats.

**NRFB: $95.00+**
**M/C: $35.00 – 45.00**

### 3371 – Super Snoozers (1972)

This set features two-piece white cotton pajamas with pale pink dots and floral print; top with elastic and lace sleeve trim, two lace-trimmed pockets, and three yellow plastic buttons; elastic waist bottoms; three yellow plastic hair rollers; yellow plastic mirror, brush, and comb; and mustard felt slippers with gold beads.

**NRFB: $50.00+**
**M/C: $20.00 – 25.00**

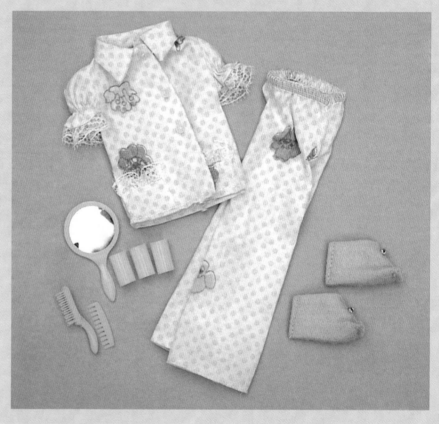

## 3372 – Fun Runners (1972)

This ensemble contains denim jeans with white stitching; yellow sleeveless tricot top; red vinyl belt with gold metal buckle; red and white calico scarf; red sunglasses; and white tennis shoes.
*This outfit is HTF.*

**NRFB: $75.00+**
**M/C: $45.00 – 55.00**

# Skipper Doll's World of Fashion

### 3373 – Flower Power (1972)
This ensemble has a red and white calico maxi skirt with ruffled hem; pink and white calico full short skirt; white cotton blouse with collar, puffed sleeves, and three buttons; red velveteen belt with black braid ties (VHTF); and red Taiwan flats.

**NRFB: $60.00+**
**M/C: $25.00 – 35.00**

### 3374 – White, Bright 'n Sparkling (1972)
This set contains a white pique maxi coat with gold braid waist trim and six gold bead buttons; matching shoulder bag with long gold chain and gold braid trim; and white Taiwan flats.

**NRFB: $25.00+**
**M/C: $15.00**

**Best Buy Era
Fashions**

# Skipper Doll's World of Fashion

Fashions of this era are lumped in the overall category of "Best Buy" because of the title used on the packaging. However other packaging titles included "Get–Ups 'n Go," "Fashion Originals," and "Growing Up Fashions." It is not unusual to find the same outfit in different packaging styles.

No longer considered the Mod era, clothing from this period is not of the highest quality. Many pieces are not hemmed or lined, the clothing is not tagged, and the finishing is usually crude. Because of the inferior workmanship of these items, many of them are fragile, and it is difficult to find them in complete and mint condition. Although most collectors have nothing but disdain for the clothing from this era, there are some charming ensembles that often include multiple pieces and early style accessories. Many of the outfits are far less interesting than the packaging graphics, especially the graphics in the Get-Ups 'n Go line. As a rule, outfits labeled "Best Buy" did not come with shoes even though Mattel catalogs and fashion booklets show the dolls wearing them.

## 8610 – Best Buy Fashion (1973)

This pale yellow maxi dress with ruffled hem, pink and blue rickrack trim, and attached white blouse is HTF in mint condition.

### NRFB: $40.00+; M/C: $10.00

## 8611– Best Buy Fashion (1973)

This outfit includes a dress with white tricot, long-sleeved top stitched in navy with navy necktie; skirt of navy with red, white, and yellow floral print; red knit vest; and white tricot kneesocks.

### NRFB: $45.00+
### M/C: $15.00 – 20.00

## 8612 – Best Buy Fashion (1973)

This set includes a pink floral print flannel robe with pink tricot collar and tie; and a sleeveless pink tricot nightgown with lace trim around yoke and two pearl buttons.

**NRFB: $45.00**
**M/C: $15.00 – 20.00**

## 8613 – Best Buy Fashion (1973)

This ensemble features a red flannel coat with white faux fur trim at collar and hem; matching faux fur trimmed hat; and red vinyl belt with gold metal ring buckle (VHTF).

**NRFB: $50.00; M/C: $20.00 – 25.00**

### 7713 – "Super dreamy for sleep-over parties!"
### Get-Ups 'n Go (1973 – 1974)

This fashion set contains two-piece pajamas of floral and dot print fabric: bottoms are footed and top has eyelet trim and gathered cuffs; lime green night cap with eyelet trim; sleeping bag of pink floral print with lime green lining and eyelet trim; four pink hair rollers; lime green plastic comb and brush; and white furry cat with hot pink neck ribbon.

### NRFB: $50.00+; M/C: $30.00 – 40.00

### 8624 – Best Buy Fashion (1973)

This set has four "Skipper" hangers and eight pairs of Taiwan flats: royal, white, burgundy, forest green, hot pink, orange, black, and yellow.

### NRFB: $50.00+

### 7714 – "Pink & pretty fashions for ballet class!"
### Get-Ups 'n Go (1973 – 1974)

This ensemble includes pink tights and leotard; pink jacket with princess yoke, smocking, and light pink ribbon collar and tie; white satin tutu with white and silver tulle skirt; pink satin ballet bag; pink plastic comb and brush; and pink ballet slippers with pink cord ties.
*This outfit is HTF.*

### NRFB: $60.00+; M/C: $35.00 – 45.00

## 7715 – "Fun clothes for the great outdoors!"
### Get-Ups 'n Go (1973)

This set contains a blue denim chambray jacket stitched in red; matching chambray shorts and hat; short-sleeved shirt with brown print; brown vinyl backpack; sleeping bag of blue and white striped fabric with orange flannel lining; light blue cotton kneesocks; and white tennis shoes.

### NRFB: $45.00+; M/C: $25.00 – 35.00

## 7770 – Best Buy Fashion (1974)

This set features red Pepsi-Cola-print pants with elastic waist; white short-sleeved crop top, with two waist ruffles of Pepsi-Cola-print; plastic hamburger; and plastic bottle of "Pepsi."

\*This outfit is VHTF.\*

### NRFB: $60.00+; M/C: $50.00 – 60.00

## 1513 – Young Ideas (Sears Exclusive) (1974)

A new version of Young Ideas was created this year using different fabrics. Major changes to the Sears exclusive ensemble are: deletion of the present, party invitation, granny glasses, jump rope, and ball; a V-neck, knit bodyshirt substituted for the knit shirt; opaque tights substituted for sheer pantyhose; and the two pieces of the cropped top playsuit's fabric do not match. As with the earlier version, the variations to this set are probably unlimited.

## 7771 – Best Buy Fashion (1974)

This ensemble includes a Hawaiian print sundress with solid pink ruffled cap sleeves and hem and matching print panties (HTF).

**NRFB: $50.00+**
**M/C: $15.00 – 20.00**

## 7772 – Best Buy Fashion (1974)

This set contains white pants with elastic waist and a blue and white print jacket with white collar and cuffs with blue buttons.

**NRFB: $45.00+; M/C: $15.00 – 20.00**

# Skipper Doll's World of Fashion

### 7773 – Best Buy Fashion (1974)
This set includes a dress with white bodice, two red buttons, attached red vest, and navy floral skirt; and white tricot slip with ruffled hem.
*This outfit is VHTF.*

**NRFB: $45.00+**
**M/C: $30.00 – 40.00**

### 7774 – Best Buy Fashion (1974)
This ensemble contains a long jumper dress of red with blue and yellow floral print and a white tricot blouse with lace-trimmed sleeves and collar, and red tie at neck.

**NRFB: $40.00+**
**M/C: $10.00**

### 7775 – Best Buy Fashion (1974)
This set showcases a white long-sleeved maxi dress with yellow and pink floral print, ruffled yoke, and black ribbon trim at gathered cuffs and waist.

**NRFB: $40.00+**
**M/C: $10.00**

## 7847 – "Flower girl flair so prettily!"
### Get-Ups 'n Go (1974 – 1976)

This ensemble features a yellow nylon long dress with yellow dotted Swiss overdress and white pouf sleeves, white ribbon waistband with long ties, and flower accent; white textured pinafore; yellow tulle headband with three flowers; bouquet of three flowers with yellow tulle and white cord ties; and white Taiwan flats.

**NRFB: $50.00+**
**M/C: $25.00 – 35.00**

### 7848 – "Beachy bits for sunny fun!" Get-Ups 'n Go (1974 – 1975)

This set has a two-piece red tricot swimsuit; multicolored print pants with elastic waist; matching long dress with yellow tricot halter top; matching headband; red and yellow color-block tricot halter top (elastic waist); white cotton elastic waist shorts with pocket; yellow tricot hankie (in shorts pocket); yellow terrycloth beach towel; orange plastic snorkel; orange plastic swim mask; and orange plastic swim fins.

**NRFB: $60.00+**
**M/C: $25.00 – 35.00**

### 9021 –  Growing Up Fashion (1975 – 1976)

This ensemble features red elastic waist pants; red and white striped crop tank top; red and white striped tank top with elastic waist; blue, short cotton skirt with white stitching; red and white striped kneesocks; red and white jump rope; blue plastic transistor radio; and white flats.

**NRFB: $35.00+; M/C: $25.00 – 27.00**

## 9022 – Growing Up Fashion
## (1975 – 1976)

This fashion set contains floral print pants with elastic waist; matching V-neck crop top with cap sleeves; red, short full skirt with white stitching and elastic waist; red tank top with white stitching, elastic waist, and white bow accent; plastic hamburger; and red Taiwan flats.

### NRFB: $35.00+; M/C: $25.00 – 27.00

## 9023 – Growing Up Fashion
## (1975 – 1976)

This ensemble includes a red bandana-print maxi skirt with elastic waist; matching halter top; matching full, short denim skirt with red contrast stitching; white ribbed tank top; cardboard mirror with face printed on back, red Taiwan flats; and black Taiwan flats.

### NRFB: $35.00+; M/C: $25.00

### 9024 – Growing Up Fashion (1975 – 1976)

This set includes a brown, white, yellow, beige, and orange plaid maxi skirt; matching striped, short, sleeveless, tank-style dress; yellow vinyl belt with yellow buckle; orange knit sleeveless turtleneck; yellow long-sleeved knit shirt with scoop front and waist ties; brown plastic soda bottle; green "Arithmetic" book; and brown Taiwan flats.

### NRFB: $35.00; M/C: $25.00

### Growing Up Fashion "Deluxe Set"

This set combines Growing Up Fashions #9023 and #9024. Other combinations for this deluxe set may exist.

### NRFB: $50.00+

### 7250 – "Glad plaids for coming & going!"
### Get-Ups 'n Go (1975 – 1976)

This fashion ensemble contains red elastic waist pants; red, yellow, and white plaid coat with attached self-tie belt and white collar; matching plaid short skirt; white ribbed shirt; red wrap tricot blouse; and red Taiwan flats.

### NRFB: $50.00+; M/C: $25.00 – 35.00

# Skipper Doll's World of Fashion

## 7251 – Olympic Skating Get-Ups 'n Go (1975)

This ensemble features a long-sleeved tricot top of red, white, and blue; short white, skirt with inverted center pleat; blue tricot cap; red tricot tights; Olympic "gold" medal; and white ice skates with silver plastic blades. *VHTF in the "Get-Ups 'n Go" packaging.*

**NRFB: $50.00+; M/C: $35.00 – 40.00**

## 7218 – Best Buy Fashion (1975)

This set contains a red and white floral dress with white inset bodice and sleeves, white cord bow at waist.

**NRFB: $30.00**
**M/C: $8.00**

### 7220 – Best Buy Fashion (1975)

This outfit consists of one-piece, footed pink tricot pajamas with elastic waist, lace yoke and cuffs, and white collar.

**NRFB: $30.00**
**M/C: $8.00**

### 7221 – Best Buy Fashion (1975)

This fashion set features a blue denim halter top with red stitching and red braid neck trim; matching short skirt; matching sun hat; and red long-sleeved tricot shirt.

**NRFB: $40.00**
**M/C: $10.00 – 15.00**

### 7222 – Best Buy Fashion (1975)

This ensemble has blue and white striped overalls; red short-sleeved tricot T-shirt; and red floral head scarf.
*This outfit is HTF.*

**NRFB: $45.00**
**M/C: $20.00 – 25.00**

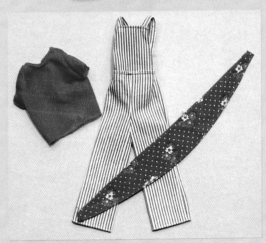

# Skipper Doll's World of Fashion

### 7223 – Best Buy Fashion (1975)

This fashion features a white tank blouse with gathered waist and loop trim at hem and straps and navy floral tricot maxi skirt.

**NRFB: $35.00+**

**M/C: $10.00 – 15.00**

### 7274 – Best Buy Fashion (1975)

This set contains a red, white, and blue tricot swimsuit; red, white, and blue striped terrycloth towel; and Olympic "gold" medal.

*This outfit is VHTF NRFB.*

**NRFB: $60.00+**

**M/C: $20.00 – 30.00**

### 9512 – Growing Up Fashion (1976)

This ensemble showcases a pink tricot blouse with lace-trimmed, puffed sleeves and lace yoke; pink tricot skirt with elastic waist and ruffle at hem; pale yellow tricot tank top with lace bodice trim; maxi skirt of three tiers: pink, pale yellow, and pale blue tricot, each trimmed with lace; white paper invitation with maroon text; and yellow cardboard present (flat) with yellow ribbon.

*This outfit is VHTF.*

**NRFB: $55.00+**

**M/C: $25.00 – $30.00**

### 9513 – Growing Up Fashion (1976)

This set contains a yellow elastic-ribbed tank top accented with green stitching and ruffled peplum; lime green and orange color-blocked skirt with elastic waist, accented with yellow front stripe; wrap waist blouse of green and orange color blocks with yellow shawl collar, waist, and ties; lime green elastic waist pants; yellow cardboard present (flat) with green ribbon; and white paper invitation with maroon text (not shown).

**NRFB: $55.00+; M/C: $30.00 – 35.00**

### 9165 – "Bicentennial fashions – patriotic & pretty." Get-Ups 'n Go (1976)

This outfit showcases a maxi dress with red skirt with Revolutionary War soldiers printed around hem, attached white blouse with leg of mutton sleeves and lace trim; blue cotton lace-up vest with white cord ties, white cotton bloomers with lace hem trim, and navy blue bows; red bag with Colonial flag decal and white drawstrings; white cotton mob cap; and navy blue Taiwan flats.
*This outfit is VHTF.*

**NRFB: $75.00+; M/C: $40.00 – 50.00**

# Skipper Doll's World of Fashion

## 9166 – "Warm weather weekend wardrobe." Get-Ups 'n Go (1976)

This ensemble includes a red, white, and blue plaid jumper with two blue button accents; matching pants with elastic waist; long-sleeved blue tricot blouse with white collar and cuffs; blue tricot cap; white tricot bra and panties (RARE); white tricot kneesocks; and white tennis shoes.
*This outfit is VHTF.*

**NRFB: $75.00+**
**M/C: $45.00 – 50.00**

## 9121 – Best Buy Fashion (1976)

This fashion contains a red and white plaid coat with black collar and three black buttons; matching tam with black ribbon trim; and black velveteen belt with red plastic buckle (HTF).
*This outfit is HTF.*
*This fashion matches Best Buy #9122.*

**NRFB: $40.00+; M/C: $20.00**

## 9122 – Best Buy Fashion (1976)

This ensemble includes a red and white plaid A-line skirt; black velveteen vest with two red buttons and red stitching; and white short-sleeved blouse with collar (HTF).
*This fashion matches Best Buy #9121.*

**NRFB: $45.00+; M/C: $20.00**

## 9123 – Best Buy Fashion (1976)
This outfit features a blue and white calico maxi dress with ruffled hem and white ribbon waist bow; and white short-sleeved blouse with lace trim at cuffs and collar.

### NRFB: $35.00
### M/C: $8.00

## 9124 – Best Buy Fashion (1976)

This patriotic outfit includes a short-sleeved, red tricot shirt with Colonial flag decal; white cotton elastic waist pants with red stitching; and white cotton cap with blue vinyl bill.

**NRFB: $40.00+**
**M/C: $15.00**

# Skipper Doll's World of Fashion

### 9125 – Best Buy Fashion (1976)
This pistachio, pink, and black calico granny dress with black bow at neck has an attached white cotton lace-trimmed apron.

**NRFB: $35.00**
**M/C: $8.00**

### 9746 – "Lacey charmer & partytimer."
### Get-Ups 'n Go (1977)
This ensemble features a long-sleeved, full-length cotton dress with pale blue skirt with ruffle, white bodice with lace collar and trim, and black grosgrain ribbon waistband and accent bow; pale blue cotton bonnet with white lace trim and black grosgrain ribbon trim and streamers; white full-length tricot slip with ruffle; and black Taiwan flats.

**NRFB: $40.00+**
**M/C: $15.00 – 20.00**

### 9126 – Best Buy Fashion (1976)
This outfit includes a red maxi skirt with hem ruffle and patriotic print; matching red print head scarf; and white sleeveless smock with red rickrack yoke, red grosgrain ties (in back), and loop trim at hem.

**NRFB: $40.00+; M/C: $15.00 – 20.00**

## 9747 – "Red set for when it's wet."
## Get-Ups 'n Go (1977)

This ensemble includes a long-sleeved dress with red, white, and blue checked knit bodice, blue collar, and elastic waistband, red cotton skirt with white stitching; red and clear vinyl raincoat with white stitching, two pockets, and two white buttons; matching vinyl rain hat and school bag; cardboard green "Arithmetic" book; cardboard yellow "English" book; and red-orange Taiwan flats.

## NRFB: $60.00+; M/C: $30.00 – 40.00

## 9748 – "For schooltime, playtime, anytime."
## Get-Ups 'n Go (1977)

This outfit features red cotton pants; white tricot short-sleeved blouse with collar and elastic waistband; red, blue, and green zigzag-striped knit jacket with red knit collar and waistband and blue cotton sleeves; matching red, blue, and green zigzag-striped knit cap; sleeveless dress; red, blue, and green zigzag-striped bodice, blue cotton skirt with center pleat and red stitching, and red vinyl belt with blue plastic buckle; white tricot knee-high socks; and red-orange Taiwan flats.

## NRFB: $50.00+; M/C: $30.00 – 35.00

### 9706 – Best Buy Fashion (1977)

This fashion has a light blue denim skirt with center pleat and blue stitching; matching denim shorts; and navy tricot short-sleeved top with rainbow decal.

*This outfit is HTF.*

**NRFB: $40.00+**
**M/C: $15.00 – 20.00**

### 9707 – Best Buy Fashion (1977)

This red and white cotton full-length dress with white bodice has a matching lace-trimmed head scarf with red ties.

**NRFB: $15.00**
**M/C: $8.00**

### 9708 – Best Buy Fashion (1977)
This outfit features a blue and green abstract-print knit dress with white tricot long sleeves and yoke; blue knit cap; and white tricot knee-high socks.
*This outfit is HTF.*

**NRFB: $45.00+; M/C: $20.00 – $30.00**

### 9709 – Best Buy Fashion (1977)
This ensemble includes a white cotton halter top with white lace trim and black accent bow at waist and a pastel green taffeta full-length skirt.

**NRFB: $40.00; M/C: $15.00**

### 9710 – Best Buy Fashion (1977)
This set has a sleeveless dress with blue cotton bodice, two white buttons, and multi-striped brown tricot skirt; and white tricot short-sleeved blouse.
*This is our vote for the most hideous Skipper outfit ever produced.*

**NRFB: $40.00; M/C: $5.00**

### 2231 – Best Buy Fashion
### (1978)

This blue and white cotton full-length skirt has a matching halter top with white lace trim.
**Variation:** Both pieces in red cotton fabric with blue, gold, and white horses, and flowers.

**NRFB: $45.00+**
**M/C: $10.00 – 15.00**

### 2232 – Best Buy Fashion
### (1978)

This outfit contains a yellow full-length dress with elastic waist and black, orange, and green print bodice and skirt trim.

**NRFB: $35.00**
**M/C: $8.00**

### 9711 – Best Buy Fashion
### (1977)

This is a pink cotton full-length dress with white lace trim at yoke and skirt hem, and black grosgrain ribbon bow accent at yoke.

**NRFB: $35.00**
**M/C: $8.00**

**skipper**®

### 2233 – Best Buy Fashion (1978)
This outfit is a red, white, and blue floral print halter jumpsuit.

**NRFB: $35.00**
**M/C: $8.00**

### 2234 – Best Buy Fashion (1978)

This outfit features an empire waist maxi dress with white cotton bodice and red and white floral print skirt, and a white vinyl purse.

**NRFB: $35.00; M/C: $8.00**

### 2235 – Best Buy Fashion (1978)

This sleeveless yellow, blue, orange, and black print sundress comes with yellow tricot head scarf (VHTF).

**NRFB: $35.00; M/C: $8.00**

### 2236 – Best Buy Fashion (1978)

Here is a fuchsia tricot sundress with shoulder straps and shirred bodice.

**NRFB: $30.00; M/C: $8.00**

### 2237 – Best Buy Fashion (1978)

This outfit includes a red floral top with elastic waist and blue braid trim; blue skirt with red stitching; and white vinyl sun visor (RARE).

**NRFB: $40.00+**
**M/C: $10.00 – 15.00**

### 2284 – Heubsch Kombiniert (1978) – Europe

This fashion set features a rose satin cape with white faux fur collar, white ribbon ties, and white loop trim; matching dress with navy velveteen, lace-up bodice (hot pink cord ties), and overskirt of sheer "diamond print" nylon; hot pink tricot slip with lace trim; hot pink tricot panties; rose satin drawstring bag; and hot pink Taiwan flats.
*This outfit is HTF.*

**NRFB: $95.00+; M/C: $50.00 – 60.00**

### 9931 – Fashion Originals (1977) – Europe

This ensemble showcases a denim jacket with yellow stitching, three yellow buttons, and red calico yoke patches; matching denim pants with red calico flower decal; red calico sleeveless blouse with shirred waist and ruffled collar; red elastic waist skirt with red calico flower decal; red tricot scarf; and red Taiwan flats.
*This outfit is HTF.*

**NRFB: $75.00+; M/C: $50.00 – 60.00**

### 2307 – "Flower Girl" Get-Ups 'n Go (1978)

This set has a yellow taffeta, empire-waist gown with sheer floral print overlay and yellow ribbon waist accent; matching bonnet; bouquet of flowers: green tricot base, yellow and green plastic flowers, and yellow ribbon bow; and yellow Taiwan flats.
*This outfit is RARE.*

**NRFB: $50.00+; M/C: $30.00 – 35.00**

## 2286 – Mollig Warm (1978) – Europe

This fashion set includes a navy hooded parka with white faux fur trim; blue and white checked jumpsuit with yellow tricot turtleneck insert and cuffs; attached white vinyl belt and wallet; and yellow Taiwan flats.
*This outfit is HTF.*

**NRFB: $75.00+**
**M/C: $50.00 – 60.00**

## 2285 – Blumenmadchen
## (1978) – Europe

This outfit includes an orange and red floral, long-sleeved dress with white collar, navy braid necktie and trim; red-orange sleeveless cotton dress with navy stitching; navy velveteen vest with red rickrack trim; red fleece beret; gold felt shoulder wallet with navy braid straps; white tricot kneesocks; and red Taiwan flats.
*This outfit is HTF.*

**NRFB: $75.00+**
**M/C: $50.00 – 60.00**

# Skipper Doll's World of Fashion

## Sample and Prototype Fashions

Mattel designers are constantly creating fashions that are not selected for production. To collectors these seem just as wonderful as those fashions actually produced, sometimes even better, and there doesn't seem to be a good reason why they were not manufactured. Although we will never know why some fashions were chosen instead of others, it is still fun to see the creative directions that Skipper doll's wardrobe might have taken.

When purchasing prototypes and samples, it is important to have as much documentation about their origin as possible. Many times, original sample tags or stickers will still be attached to the garments to prove their authenticity. When found with proper documentation, these unique pieces usually command top dollar and are impossible to assign a value to.

The following prototypes we have named ourselves and were never produced as shown.

*A selection of adorable swimsuits is pictured. The swimsuit second from the left was supposedly designed for a black Skipper doll that was never produced.*

Collection of Alana Brandstrom

## Oodles of Poodles

Obviously intended as a companion sister fashion for Barbie doll's #1643 Poodle Parade, this outfit would certainly have taken best of show in the hearts of collectors. The Poodle was created by David Escobedo.

And even more prototype swimsuits! The suit at the far right is pieced and sewn. If it had made it into production, the suit would have been a printed material.

Collection of Leslie Bote

A sample of the 1968 Twist 'n Turn Skipper swimsuit made with a ruffle of Francie's #1211 Tenterrific.

Collection of Leslie Bote

# Skipper Doll's World of Fashion

### Goody Goody Gum Drops!
A yummy variation of #1912 Cookie Time.

### Pretty Midi
An unusual fabric variation of #1974 Eeny Meeny Midi, missing the yellow waist bow.

### Color Shift
A pretty little shift dress, which would have been more interesting with its accessories.

Collection of Cheryl Nelson

### Rosy Posies
A beautiful pastel version of #1955 Posy Party.

Collection of Judy Schizas

### Field Flowers and Lazy Days
Two beautiful and simple dresses for Skipper doll. There is a matching prototype ensemble for Barbie doll in the Field Flowers material, consisting of a granny dress and ruffled shawl.

### Check it Out!
A cute sample of Get Ups 'n Go #9748 – For schooltime, playtime, anytime. The skirt was not included in the production version.

### Stripes and Chex
An unsightly combination of knits was used to create this prototype matching dress and cardigan.

### Ruffled Up
A multi-tiered, ruffled party dress in cotton pique.

Collection of Judy Schizas

### Pretty in Velvet
A beautiful sample of #3477 Dressed in Velvet, made of turquoise velveteen instead of the production fabric of rose velveteen.

A packaging sample of #3295 Turn Abouts.

A packaging sample of #3478 Long 'n Short of It.

### Little Girl Blue
A sample `of Best Buy #8613. The coat has a slightly fuller cut and hand-painted buttons.

### Summer Sojourn
A darling little sample that was not mass produced. The accompanying paperwork indicates it was approved and intended for production. It may have been sold on the foreign market.

# Chapter 4
# Tutti & Todd
# Dolls' World

# Tutti & Todd Dolls' World

Mattel added another family member to Barbie doll's world in 1966. Smaller than Skipper doll, she was Tutti, the tiny little sister of Barbie and Skipper. Tutti doll was successful enough for Mattel to add her tiny twin brother, Todd, in 1967, as well as their adorable little friend Chris. A unique wire armature inside the doll's body allowed the arms and legs to be posed in unlimited positions. Many of the dolls found today have turned green because of the chemical reaction between the wire skeleton and the vinyl, or the wire has broken through the vinyl skin. For safety reasons, this may have contributed to the discontinuation of the doll in 1972 in the United States.

Unlike the introduction of Skipper doll's fashions, Tutti's ensembles did not match either Skipper or Barbie doll's fashions. However many fabrics used with Barbie, Ken and Skipper fashions were recycled with Tutti and Todd fashions.

## U.S. Market
### 3550 – Tutti (1966)

Tutti has a two-piece sunsuit of pink cotton gingham (large or small print) with a white ruffle and floral appliqués. She has a matching sun hat, pink grosgrain hair band, "Tutti" booklet, pink plastic comb and brush, and white plastic strap or bow flats. She was produced in either blonde or "brownette" and the box is printed as such. Research indicates that these first Tutti dolls did not come with wrist tags.

> Markings:
> ©1965
> MATTEL. INC.
> Japan

### NRFB $175.00 – 195.00; M/C: $60.00

### 3580 – Tutti (1967 – 1971)

Tutti doll got a new empire-waist sundress with attached panties this year. Blonde dolls came with a floral skirt and a hot pink bodice accented with a yellow ribbon, and brunette dolls wore the reverse. Her accessories are pink grosgrain hair band, pink plastic comb and brush, booklet, and white plastic bow flats. Other noticeable changes are a slightly larger box in red, orange, and hot pink, and a "Tutti" wrist tag.
**Variation:** The sundress bodice was also produced in a rose-print fabric.

> Markings:
> ©1965
> MATTEL. INC.
> Japan

### NRFB: $200.00+; M/C: $65.00

# Tutti & Todd Dolls' World

### 3590 – Todd (1967 – 1968)

Tutti's tiny twin brother was just adorable in his dark blue shirt and red, white, and blue plaid shorts and cap. He has brown eyes and was available in red hair only. His accessories include dark blue knit socks, red vinyl oxfords, plastic comb and brush, booklet, and wrist tag. A rare NRFB dressed Todd doll was discovered wearing #3556 Sundae Treat. It is believed this was an overstock item re-packaged and sold at the Mattel store.

> Markings:
> ©1965
> MATTEL. INC.
> Japan

### NRFB: $200.00+; M/C: $60.00

### 3552 – Walkin' My Dolly (1966 – 1968)

This set contains an ash blonde ponytail Tutti doll in a sleeveless cotton sundress. The bodice is white with red flocked polka dots, and the skirt is red with white rickrack trim (similar to Buffy doll's dress, however Tutti doll's skirt is shorter and fuller). She has matching white with red flocked polka dot panties; a straw hat with red satin ribbon band and streamers accented with white bead-centered flowers; pink plastic comb and brush; white tricot socks; red vinyl oxfords; pink plastic baby carriage with white trim; plastic brown-haired baby doll with painted blue hairbow wrapped in blue flannel; and lace trimmed blanket.

**Variation:** Red and white striped fabric may be substituted for white with red polka dot fabric.

### NRFB: $300.00; M/C: $150.00+

### 3553 – Night Night Sleep Tight (1966 – 1968)

This is a titian Tutti doll with hair tied back with pale pink ribbon. She has a pink cotton empire-waist nightgown with lace trim; pink cotton floral robe with lace trim and pink ribbon necktie; pink plastic comb and brush; two-tone pink felt scuffs with ribbon and lace accent; and white plastic bed with bedspread that matches her robe.

### NRFB: $250.00 – 275.00; M/C: $150.00+

*This set was also produced in a variation fabric that is the same material used in the bassinet of #953 Barbie Babysits.*

### 3554 – Me and My Dog (1966 – 1968)

This brunette Tutti doll with red hairbow models a white faux fur bonnet with white grosgrain ribbon ties and a red felt coat with white faux fur collar and cuff, and white contrasting stitching and four clear buttons. She wears red or red and white striped knit tights and comes with a white plastic comb and brush; white vinyl oxfords; and a white fluffy dog with black bead eyes and nose, red felt mouth, and attached red cord leash.

**NRFB: $300.00; M/C: $150.00+**

### 3555 – Melody in Pink (1966 – 1968)

This blonde Tutti doll has pigtails tied with pale pink hairbows and a pale pink dress with tiers of white dotted tulle and two pale-pink bow accents. She comes with pale pink matching panties; short white tricot socks; pale pink plastic comb and brush; white strap flats or white or pale pink bow flats; and an orange plastic piano and piano bench. **Variation:** The dress was also produced in dark pink tricot with white dotted tulle tiers.

**NRFB: $300.00; M/C: $150.00+**

### 3556 – Sundae Treat (1966 – 1968)

This is the only play set that features Tutti and Todd dolls together. The titian Tutti doll sports a navy hair ribbon; a red and white striped cotton dress with white yoke trimmed in navy, a navy accent bow and three navy shank buttons; navy cotton panties; short white tricot socks; red bow flats; The titian Todd doll features a red and white striped cotton blazer with two clear buttons; white cotton short-sleeved shirt; navy cotton shorts; navy knit knee-high socks; and white or red vinyl oxfords.

The play set includes a pink plastic parlor table with metal legs and supports for two pink plastic seats; one strawberry sundae and one chocolate sundae; two metal spoons; and a turquoise plastic comb and brush.

**NRFB: $350.00 – 400.00**
**M/C: $200.00+**

### 3559 – Cookin' Goodies (1967 – 1968)

This brunette Tutti doll with up-swept hairdo wears a yellow long-sleeved dress with orange and white floral print. The collar and skirt hem is either solid orange or solid yellow fabric. She also wears a white grosgrain ribbon bow at her neck and a white lace-trimmed apron with grosgrain ribbon ties.

This set includes a pink plastic comb and brush; short white tricot socks; orange bow flats; white plastic stove with black burners, pink "Tutti" painted logo and additional pink painted details (optional); and a pink plastic saucepan with black handle.

**NRFB: $340.00; M/C: $175.00+**

### 3560 – Swing-A-Ling (1967 – 1968)

This ash blonde Tutti doll wears a green hairband accented with two orange flowers; a yellow taffeta dress with white lace, and a green grosgrain ribbon waistband with orange flower accent; and short yellow tricot socks. She comes with a white plastic comb and brush; white bow **or** strap flats; and a white plastic swing with orange plastic seat.
*This set is VHTF.*

**NRFB: $350.00 – 400.00; M/C: $250.00+**

### 3570 – Chris (1967 – 1971)

Tutti's brown-eyed friend was available in either blonde or brunette (it is difficult to find brunette dolls that have not oxidized to one of the various shades of red). She wore a mod print sundress and green cotton panties. Her accessories include a green metal barrette, two green grosgrain hair bows, plastic comb and brush, booklet, and orange bow flats.

| Markings: |
| --- |
| ©1965 |
| MATTEL, INC. |
| Japan |

**NRFB: $200.00 – 225.00; M/C: $75.00**

## 3301 – Chris Fun-Timers Set
## (Sears Exclusive) (1967)

The standard Chris doll and original outfit came in this set, which also included a silver lamé sleeveless dress trimmed in hot pink nylon; matching hot pink nylon shorts, red and pink swirl-print oilcloth pantsuit trimmed in white cord (pants have attached belt with metal buckle); matching oilcloth cap; hot pink and yellow sleeveless cotton dress with "doll" decal; clear vinyl sleeveless dress with hot pink vertical stripes; hot pink vinyl shoulder bag; short white tricot socks; white vinyl boots; and hot pink bow flats.

### NRFB: $850.00+; M/C: $400.00

Collections of Priscilla Wardlow and Kevin Dickson

Collections of Priscilla Wardlow and Kevin Dickson

## 3577 – Buffy & Mrs. Beasley (1968 – 1970)

Portrayed by child actress Anissa Jones on television's *Family Affair,* Buffy was never without her trusted friend, Mrs. Beasley. Buffy wears a sleeveless cotton sundress. The bodice is white with red flocked polka dots, and the attached skirt is red cotton trimmed in white rickrack. She also has white with red polka dot panties; two red hair ribbons; short white tricot socks; and red vinyl oxfords with white soles. Mrs. Beasley has a one-piece body of aqua and white polka dot fabric with the waistband and collar trimmed in yellow rickrack, and yellow ribbon ties at the neck. Her "hands" are pink felt, her "feet" are yellow felt, and she wears a pair of hard-to-find black plastic granny glasses (these are the same glasses found in some Francie doll and Skipper doll ensembles).

| Markings: |
| --- |
| ©1965 |
| MATTEL, INC. |
| Japan |

### NRFB: $225.00 – 250.00; M/C: $125.00

Chapter 4

## Pretty Pairs (1970)

These Tutti-sized dolls were sold in blister packaging and available in 1970 only. Each doll came with a silver "Japan" wrist tag and was promoted as being able to wear Tutti doll's clothing ensembles.

> Markings:
> ©1965
> MATTEL. INC.
> Japan

### NRFB: $200.00 each; M/C: $150.00 each

### 1133 – Lori 'n Rori

This blonde doll with pink hairbow wears a pink, white, and blue floral and striped cotton dress trimmed in hot pink ribbon, rickrack, and lace. She has short white tricot socks and hot pink bow flats, and carries a brown fuzzy teddy bear with hot pink ribbon tie at neck.

### 1134 – Nan 'n Fran

This African-American doll wears a floral flannel nightgown trimmed with lace and green ribbon bows. She has a pink flannel, lace-trimmed nightcap and pink felt scuffs with white lace flowers and green bead centers. Her matching doll wears hot pink flannel pajamas trimmed at the neck with lace and green ribbon.

### 1135 – Angie 'n Tangie

This brunette doll with side ponytail tied with hot pink ribbon wears a sleeveless orange full-skirted dress trimmed with white lace and hot pink ribbon. She has white fishnet tights and hot pink bow flats, and carries a matching rag doll with yellow yarn hair and a hot pink outfit trimmed with lace and orange ribbon.

# Tutti & Todd Dolls' World

## Tutti Doll Fashions (U.S. Market)

### 3601 – Puddle Jumpers (1966)
This set includes a blue textured vinyl raincoat with blue floral laminated lining, white stitching and three buttons; matching rain hat; and white vinyl boots.
**NRFB: $65.00; M/C: $25.00**

### 3602 – Ship Shape (1966)
This set features a sleeveless aqua sailor dress with white polka dots, front pleat, white collar, and red grosgrain accent bow; matching panties; white cotton sailor's hat with red pompon; short white tricot socks; and white bow flats.
**NRFB: $95.00; M/C: $45.00**

### 3603 – Sand Castles (1966)
Sand Castles contains a white cotton sunsuit with red polka dots and red grosgrain accent bow at waist; matching sun hat with red grosgrain ties; red plastic bucket with handle and sailboat decal; metal shovel with red handle; and red strap flats.
**NRFB: $95.00; M/C: $45.00**

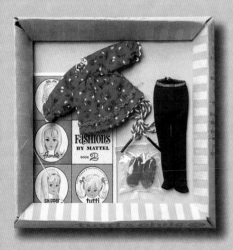

### 3604 – Skippin' Rope (1966)
This set has a red, white, green, and blue cotton floral dress with green and white rickrack trim; navy stretch tights; a white and red jump rope with black handles; and red vinyl oxfords or bow flats.
**NRFB: $75.00 – 150.00**
**M/C: $40.00 – 60.00**
(variation commands the high value)
**Variation:** Dress was also produced in the same floral print as Barbie doll's "On The Go" Pak.

157

# Tutti & Todd Dolls' World

### 3606 – Clowning Around (1967)
This ensemble features a cotton dress with black and white checked full skirt and yellow long-sleeved bodice; large white bow at the neck and wide white cuffs at wrists; yellow cotton panties; clown doll with matching checked pants and hat, yellow felt torso, arms and feet, and white pompon head with black felt eyes and nose and red mouth; and black bow flats.

### NRFB: $100.00; M/C: $65.00

### 3607 – Come to My Party (1967)
This fashion set includes a light blue organdy sleeveless party dress with light blue taffeta lining; bodice in white lace with pink flowers and green ribbon accents; light blue taffeta panties; short white tricot socks; and white bow flats.

### NRFB: $100.00; M/C: $45.00

### 3609 – Plantin' Posies (1967)
Plantin' Posies contains a yellow and orange cotton sleeveless sundress with daisy accent decals; yellow cotton panties; orange cotton sun hat with yellow cotton ties and daisy decals; green plastic watering can with matching lid; green plastic trowel; white paper "Seed" pack with green printing; and orange bow flats.

### NRFB: $100.00; M/C: $65.00

### 3614 – Sea-Shore Shorties
### (1968 – 1969)
This ensemble includes a lime green and blue floral cotton sleeveless sundress with three rows of white eyelet ruffles; matching two-piece bikini; blue plastic toy sailboat with white plastic sail; green and yellow plastic beachball; and white bow flats.

### NRFB: $95.00; M/C: $65.00

# Tutti & Todd Dolls' World

### 3615 – Flower Girl (1968 – 1969)
This ensemble includes a full-length empire-waist gown with bodice in aqua satin edged with white loop trim, yellow velveteen flower with bead center and white satin bow accent at waist; skirt in white taffeta with white organdy overskirt trimmed with aqua satin ribbon and embroidered flowers; aqua satin headband with yellow net and flower trim; basket of yellow and aqua flowers with yellow elastic handle, white lace and yellow satin ribbon; and white bow flats.
### NRFB: $150.00 – 175.00; M/C: $125.00

### 3616 – Pinky P.J.'s (1968 – 1969)
This outfit features pink nylon sleeveless pajamas with white lace trim and turquoise flower accent; plastic molded baby doll; pink fleece bunting with white lace trim (lace is different than pajamas); turquoise plastic comb and brush; and dark pink felt scuffs.
### NRFB: $100.00; M/C: $85.00

### 3617 – Birthday Beauties (1968 – 1969)
This fashion set comes with a pink cotton long-sleeved party dress with daisy print; white fishnet tights; gold wrapped present with white ribbon and pink flower accent; pink plastic plate; white Styrofoam slice of cake with two painted pink stripes; white paper invitation with maroon print; pink crepe paper party favor with gold glitter; and white strap flats.
### NRFB: $125.00; M/C: $95.00

### 3608 – Let's Play Barbie (1967)
This set contains a sleeveless cotton dress with skirt in white and blue square print with red and white lace trim at hemline; bodice in solid red cotton; red cotton panties; matching red and lace-trimmed hairband; miniature "Barbie" doll; red plastic case with an "American Girl Barbie" doll decal; short white tricot socks; and white bow flats.
**Variation:** The skirt on the dress has been produced in fabric from Skipper doll's #1932 Let's Play House.
### NRFB: $195.00; M/C: $125.00

Chapter 4

# Tutti & Todd Dolls' World

## Foreign Market Tutti, Todd, Chris, and Carla Dolls

Although the Tutti-sized dolls were discontinued in the U.S. after 1971, they continued to be popular in Canada and Europe, and were produced through 1980. Mattel's 1972 German catalog shows the 1967 U.S. issues of Tutti, Todd, Chris, and Buffy and Mrs. Beasley for sale. A Mattel employee, who worked for the company during the late '60s and throughout the '70s, said it was common for Mattel to sell U.S. overstock in Europe many years after it had been discontinued. This leads us to believe that some or all of these dolls were for sale in Europe through 1974, when the new, firmer vinyl dolls exclusive to Europe were introduced to the market.

All the dolls and outfits produced for these markets are difficult to find. Carla doll was added to the line in 1976. Throughout her production, her outfit never changed. Dolls after 1974 have a smaller, firmer head, and the bodies are not easy to bend or pose. These dolls are marked Hong Kong or have no markings at all.

Outfits manufactured after 1972 recycle many of the fabrics used for Barbie, Ken, Francie, and Skipper doll ensembles. The earlier issues came packaged in the familiar U.S.-style yellow and white striped frame boxes. Beginning in 1974, the packaging style changed to a hot pink or blue window box that was sealed shut. Outfits sold in Canada and the U.K. in the yellow frame tray boxes were named in English, whereas those sold in Germany were given German names that did not translate the same as the Canadian counterparts. Our research indicates that the European and Canadian markets did not name the outfits after 1973, but referred to them only by stock number. However, those sold in Germany continued to be named and many of the names were used repeatedly for different ensembles. We have translated the German outfit names for comparison.

Collection of Paul David

Variation to #8128 Tutti (1975) — skirt and attached panties in pale yellow fabric.

Collection of Claudia Exinger

# Tutti & Todd Dolls' World

## 8128 – Tutti (1975)

Tutti doll wears an adorable yellow and orange cotton sundress with fabric from Ken doll's #1428 Breakfast at Seven. Her sundress has attached panties. Tutti wearing this hard-to-find dress was only available for one year.

**NRFB: $175.00; M/C: $100.00**

## 8128 – Tutti (1976)

Blonde Tutti doll wears an empire-waist sundress with hot pink cotton bodice, floral skirt, and attached floral panties. Waist ribbon is either yellow or aqua. Her accessories included pink plastic comb and brush, pale pink grosgrain hairband, and white bow flats. Her box is dated 1973.

**NRFB: $75.00; M/C: $50.00**

## 8128 – Tutti (1977)

Blonde re-issued Tutti doll wears a yellow sleeveless dress trimmed in white lace with a yellow accent ribbon. She has white tricot panties, a pale pink hair band, pink comb and brush, short white tricot socks, and white bow flats. Note the new hot pink box and new "Tutti" logo.

**NRFB: $65.00; M/C: $45.00**

## 8129 – Todd (1975)

This titian Todd doll was not located in time for publishing, however we do have confirmed information that this doll was produced in the outfit shown. It is identical to the 1976 Todd with the exception of the knit plaid shorts made from the same fabric as Ken's #1449 The Sea Scene.

**NRFB: $75.00+; M/C: $45.00**

## 8129 – Todd – England (1975)

Only available in England, this titian Todd doll is identical to the 1976 Todd doll, with the exception of navy and white striped knit shorts.

**NRFB: $85.00; M/C: $50.00**

## 8129 – Todd (1976)

Brunette or titian Todd doll wears a navy short sleeved shirt with two white buttons, red knit shorts, red cotton cap, short white knit socks, and white hard plastic tennis shoes (odd shaped and look more like they fit Ricky doll).

**NRFB: $75.00; M/C: $45.00**

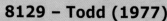

## 8129 – Todd (1977)

Brunette or titian re-issued Todd doll wears a red tricot short-sleeved shirt with blue and white checked collar, blue cotton shorts with red stitching, short white tricot socks, and blue vinyl oxfords. Note the new "Todd" logo on the box.

**NRFB: $75.00; M/C: $45.00**

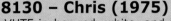

### 8130 – Chris (1975)

This Chris doll is VHTF in her red, white, and blue A-line dress and detached matching panties, made from the same material as Ken doll's #1472 The Casual Scene. The dress is tagged "Chris" on the inside. The doll and box for this year were the same as the 1967 U.S. Chris doll, with the exception of her dress. Her accessories include a green metal barrette, two green hair bows, and red or white bow flats.

**NRFB: $250.00; M/C: $150.00**

### 8130 – Chris (1976)

Titian Chris doll wears a sleeveless yellow floral sundress, with hot pink or dark green panties. Her accessories were two lime green hair bows, brass barrette, pink plastic comb and brush, and white plastic bow flats. In addition to the yellow box style shown, this same doll was also packaged in the 1967 U.S. version Chris box.

**NRFB: $150.00; M/C: $75.00**

### 8130 – Chris (1977)

Brunette Chris doll wears a new turquoise A-line dress, with white center panel and yellow edging. She was produced with two shades of auburn hair. Her accessories included white tricot panties, short white tricot socks, yellow plastic bow flats, and two hot pink hair bows. Her new "pink" box style depicts the new "Logo" typestyle Mattel began using on all logos in 1976.

**NRFB: $95.00; M/C: $65.00**

The 1975 issue of Chris came with matching panties.

Collection of Paul David

Collection of Carmen Tickal

# Tutti & Todd Dolls' World

## 7377 – Carla (1974)
This black friend doll has two pigtails tied with white grosgrain ribbons. Her orange cotton, sleeveless sundress is trimmed in white and has two patch pockets. Her accessories are white tricot panties, pink plastic comb and brush, short white tricot socks, and white bow flats.
**NRFB: $125.00; M/C: $65.00**

## 7377 – Carla (1977 – 1980)
Carla was re-issued again in 1977 with her new "pink" box style and new logo. She and her accessories remained the same as the earlier issue.
**NRFB: $125.00; M/C: $65.00**

## European Tutti Play Sets

**7453 – Tutti – New Swing-A-Ling**
**Tuttis Neue Schaukel** (Tutti's New Swing)
**NRFB $300.00 – 325.00; M/C $250.00+**

**7454 – Tutti – Walking My Dolly**
**Meine Puppe Hab Ich Lieb** (I Love My Doll)
**NRFB $300.00 – 325.00; M/C $250.00+**

**7455 – Tutti – Night Night Sleep Tight**
**Gute Nacht – Schlaf Gut** (Good Night, Sleep Well)
**NRFB $300.00 – 325.00; M/C $250.00+**

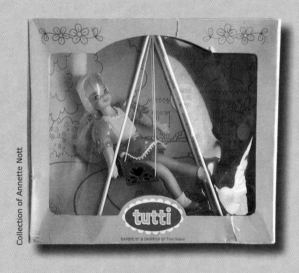

Collection of Annette Nott

Collection of Annette Nott

Collection of Annette Nott

# Tutti & Todd Dolls' World

Collection of Carmen Tickal

Collection of Priscilla Wardlow

## European Tutti and Todd Fashions

Values for clothing ensembles are for NRFB examples only. Because these outfits are so difficult to find, mint and complete outfits out of box should run 25% – 40% less than the NRFB value.

We have identified these fashions by the German name first with the English translation in parentheses, followed by the Canadian/UK (English) name if applicable.

### 8385 – Tutti – Spielkleid
### (Play Dress)
### Nice 'n Bright (1970)

This set includes a red sleeveless A-line dress with white vinyl trim, two pockets, and three red buttons; matching red panties; short white tricot socks; and red bow flats.

### NRFB: $75.00

### 8386 – Tutti – Schiff Ahoi
### (Ship Ahoy) (1970)

This set features a yellow knit turtleneck body blouse; light blue "leather" short skirt with yellow stitching; matching vest; matching sailor's cap with yellow ribbon tails; and yellow bow flats.

### NRFB: $125.00

Collection of Priscilla Wardlow

### 8387 – Tutti – Stripes 'n Slacks
### (1970)

This fashion set includes a blue and hot pink striped knit pullover with drawstring ties at waist; blue cotton bell-bottom pants with pocket and white stitching; black plastic camera; and hot pink bow flats.

### NRFB: $125.00

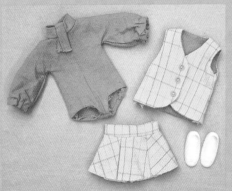

### 8388 – Tutti – Sonntagsausflug
### (Sunday Trip) (1970)

This set features a coral body blouse with attached bowtie; yellow and coral print short skirt (fabric from Ken doll's #1428 Breakfast at Seven); matching vest; and orange or white bow flats.

### NRFB: $125.00

# Tutti & Todd Dolls' World

### 8389 – Tutti – Geburtstagparty
(Birthday Party)
### Short 'n Sweet (1970)
This set includes a blue and yellow cotton long-sleeved dress; yellow cotton panties; yellow wooden yo-yo; and blue bow flats.

**NRFB: $60.00+**

### 8463 – Tutti – Grosse Ferien
(Big Holiday)
### Fringe for Fun (1971)
This set features tan flannel bell-bottom pants; brown leather-look fringe vest; lime green tricot short-sleeved top; and blue and yellow beaded headband.

**NRFB: $125.00**

### 8464 – Tutti – Mein Roter Mantel
(My Red Coat)
### Cozy Coat (1971)
This fashion ensemble features a red fleece jacket with white faux fur trim; white knitted scarf with fringe trim; and white faux fur muff.

**NRFB: $50.00**

### 8465 – Tutti – Ich Geh Spazieren
(I'm Going for a Walk)
### Cute Suit (1971)
This set includes a long-sleeved dress with navy and white striped bodice with red vinyl skirt with two pockets with navy stitching; matching vinyl vest; and white tricot panties.
**Variation:** Shown in dealer catalog with solid blue bodice.

**NRFB: $75.00**

Collection of Annette Nott

Collection of Annette Nott

Collection of Judy Schizas

Chapter 4

Collection of Annette Nott

## 8466 – Tutti – Schulausflug
### (School Trip) School Colors (1971)

This set features a blue knit drop-waist dress with short sleev
and white leather-look trim; white tricot panties; short white tric
socks; and blue bow flats.

**NRFB: $75.00**

Collection of Paul David

## 8502 – Tutti – Bequem
### und Praktisch
### (Comfortable and Practical)
### (1972)

This ensemble contains a tan
velveteen flared skirt; matching
vest; large red and blue, or small
blue and white striped long-sleeved
knit body shirt; blue knit bell-bottom
pants; and black bow flats.
**Variation:** Body shirt was also
available in orange textured knit.

**NRFB: $75.00+**

# Tutti & Todd Dolls' World

Collection of Paul David

## 8503 – Tutti – Grosse Reise
### (Big Trip) (1972)

This ensemble features a blue, red, and yellow knit skirt (fabric from Skipper doll's #1746 Wooly Winner); matching tam hat; white blouse trimmed in white lace; white panties trimmed in white lace; red vinyl vest with white cross-woven ties; red plastic suitcase; short white tricot socks trimmed in white lace; and red bow flats.

### NRFB: $95.00+

**Variation:** Skirt and hat fabric for Skipper doll's #3472 Double Dashers. German dealer catalog also shows the outfit with a yellow transistor radio instead of the red plastic suitcase.

Courtesy of 1975 Mattel German catalog

## 8505 – Tutti – Eingeladen zum Geburtstag
### (Invited to a Birthday)
## Party Velvet (1972)

This fashion set includes a full-length empire-waist dress trimmed in black with green velvet skirt and white bodice with two green buttons and long sleeves; bouquet of red, yellow, and blue flowers with lace trim; and black bow flats.

### NRFB: $95.00+

**Variation:** Blue velvet skirt has been found. In addition, there was a production sample with aqua velveteen skirt, different yellow colored trims, and pink Skipper doll flats.

Collection of Annette Nott

Production sample

## 8504 – Schnee Floeckchen
### (Snow Flakes) (1972)

This set features a light blue fleece parka with faux fur cuffs and edging, four red buttons and four pockets; white fake fur hat with red pompon; red knit tights; and white vinyl snow boots.

### NRFB: $95.00+

# Tutti & Todd Dolls' World

### 8591 – Tutti – Ich Geh Spazieren
(I'm Going for a Walk)
### Peppermint Sunday (1973)
This set includes a sleeveless white and red print sundress with red full skirt with white rickrack trim; white cotton sun hat with red grosgrain ribbon bow and trim (turns to orange; short white tricot socks; and white bow flats.

### NRFB: $95.00+

### 8592 – Tutti – Blue Jeans und Ringelpulli
(Blue Jeans and Pullover)
### Picture Perfect (1973)
This set contains blue bell-bottom cotton pants with white stitching; knit sleeveless multicolored striped pullover with drawstring ties at waist (fabric from TNT Francie swimsuit); yellow plastic transistor radio; and white bow flats.
**Variation:** Top was also produced in a white knit with fuchsia snowflake print from Francie's #3275 Little Knits.

### NRFB: $95.00+

Collection of Annette Nott

Collections of Annette Nott and Priscilla Wardlow

Collections of Annette Nott and Priscilla Wardlow

Collection of Annette Nott

### 8593 – Tutti – Ich Geh Spielen
(I Am Going to Play)
### Bloomin' Blue (1973)
This set features a blue and white checked dress with white collar and cuffs and full skirt with green rickrack trim; green knit tights; green knit cap; and white strap flats.
### NRFB: $125.00

Collection of Carmen Tickal

## 8595 – Todd – Pulli und Hose
### (Pullover and Pants) **Plaid Lad (1973)**

This set contains red and black plaid slacks (fabric from Ken do #1473 V.I.P. Scene); red long-sleeved knit top; short red knit sock and red vinyl oxfords.

**NRFB: $75.00**

Collection of Annette Nott

## 8594 – Tutti – Regentropfen
### (Raindrops)
### City Slicker (1973)

This set includes a yellow vinyl raincoat with two "pockets," two white buttons, and white stitching; matching hat; white vinyl rain boots **or** red hard plastic tennis shoes.

**NRFB: $65.00+**

## 8596 – Todd – Zum Spielplatz
### (To the Playground) **(1973)**

This ensemble comes with a cotton short-sleeved shirt with red and white vertical stripes; blue jeans with white stitching; and red cotton cap.

**NRFB: $125.00+**

# Tutti & Todd Dolls' World

### 8597 – Todd – Ausflug (A Trip)
### Checkmates (1973)

This set contains a brown and white checked long-sleeved cotton shirt (fabric from #4224 Mod Hair Ken); brown cotton shorts; gold tricot dickey; short gold tricot socks; and brown vinyl oxfords.

### NRFB: $65.00+

### 8598 – Todd – Mein Neuer Mantel
### (My New Coat) – Warm Winter (1973)

This ensemble contains a brown leather-look jacket with brown faux fur collar; red, gold, and brown long knit scarf (fabric from Ken doll's #1438 The Skiing Scene); matching knit hat; and brown vinyl rain boots.

### NRFB: $95.00+

### 7980 – Tutti – Mein Neuer Mantel
### (My New Coat) (1974)

This set comes with a red felt coat with white faux fur sleeves and two white buttons; red felt hood with white faux fur edging and white necktie; red plastic shoulder bag with bead closure; white tricot knee-high socks; and red or white bow flats.

### NRFB: $65.00+

TAIWAN

Collection of Paul David

Collection of Annette Nott

# Tutti & Todd Dolls' World

Collection of Paul David

Collection of Carmen Tickal

### 7981 – Tutti – Ich Geh Schlafen
#### (I Am Going to Sleep)
#### (1974)

This set features a pink tricot nightgown with white lace trim; pink floral print flannel robe with white lace trim and white satin ribbon ties; pink cotton nightcap with white lace trim or light pink floral flannel nightcap with lace trim; and pink scuffs with white lace trim.

**NRFB: $95.00+**

### 7982 – Tutti – Hosenanzug
#### (Pant Suit) (1974)

This ensemble includes a knit long-sleeved pullover with V-shape bodice, sleeves, and collar in yellow tricot, waistband in yellow ribbed knit, and remainder in orange and yellow knit check print (same fabric as Francie doll's #1209 Mini-Chex); matching orange and yellow knit check print pants; a yellow knit ribbed skirt; and orange bow flats.
**Variation:** Orange and yellow knit check print fabric was also substituted with solid red knit.
Note: German dealer catalog and Netherlands doll booklet each show this outfit with an orange vinyl shoulder bag.

**NRFB: $95.00+**

### 7983 – Tutti – Kinderparty
#### (Child's Party) (1974)

This set contains a pink and white dotted Swiss dress with sheer pink nylon long sleeves and white lace waistband and cuffs; matching dotted Swiss panties with white lace trim; sheer pink nylon slip with white lace trim; short white tricot socks; and white bow flats.
*This outfit is VHTF.*

**NRFB: $150.00+**

Collection of Paul David

Collection of Priscilla Wardlow

## 7984 – Todd – Jeans-Anzug
### (Jean Suit) (1974)

This set incudes a jean jacket with red stitching and three red buttons; jean pants with red stitching; and red vinyl oxfords.

**NRFB: $45.00**

## 7985 – Todd – Huebsch Angezogen
### (Well Dressed) (1974)

This ensemble comes with a white, orange, yellow, green, and blue striped cotton shirt with two white plastic buttons; white cotton shorts; white cotton sun visor; short white tricot socks; and white vinyl tennis shoes.

**NRFB: $35.00**

## 7986 – Todd – Ausflug
### (A Trip) (1974)

This set contains a blue velveteen blazer with two white plastic buttons, and white contrast stitching; matching shorts; red tricot dickey; white tricot knee-high socks; and red vinyl oxfords.

**NRFB: $45.00**

## 7987 – Todd – Sport-Fan
### (Sport Fan) (1974)

This set features a red and yellow tricot short-sleeved top; blue jeans; a red vinyl baseball cap; and red vinyl tennis shoes.

**NRFB: $45.00**

Collection of Paul David

### 7969 – Tutti – Ausflug
(A Trip) **(1975)**
This set includes a blue tricot long-sleeved body blouse with white lace trim at cuffs and collar; matching tam hat with white pompon; gold corduroy jumper with pocket and blue tricot hankie; and gold (HTF) or white tricot knee-high socks; and black bow flats.

### NRFB: $75.00+

### 7968 – Tutti – Huebsch und Praktisch
(Pretty and Practical) **(1975)**
This ensemble features a blue and white cotton long-sleeved calico-print dress; white cotton apron with lace trim; red knit tights; and red vinyl oxfords.
**Variation:** German dealer catalog and Netherlands doll booklet show a red, white, and blue floral print dress instead of the blue and white calico dress.

### NRFB: $65.00+

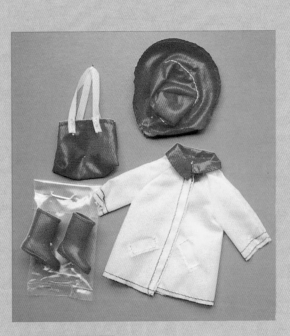

Photo courtesy of Mattel 1975 dealer catalog – European Market

00-7968
Hübsch und
praktisch

Collection of Annette Nott

### 7967 – Tutti – Regenmantel
(Rain Coat) **(1975)**
This set includes a yellow nylon rain jacket with red collar and stitching; red nylon rain hat; red nylon book bag with yellow handles; and red vinyl rain boots.

### NRFB: $45.00

# Tutti & Todd Dolls' World

### 7970 – Tutti – Gartenfest
### (Gardenfest) (1975)
This set features a white cotton sleeveless halter-top with white lace trim and white grosgrain ribbon neck and waist ties; full-length red with white paisley-print skirt with white lace edging; matching head scarf with red grosgrain ribbon ties; matching panties with white lace trim; and white bow flats.

### NRFB: $65.00+

Collection of Priscilla Wardlow

### 7971 – Todd – Fur Kuehle Tage
### (For Cold Days) (1975)
The ensemble features a red fleece hooded sweatshirt with ties; gold corduroy shorts; gold tricot knee-high socks (HTF); and brown vinyl oxfords.

### NRFB: $45.00+

### 7973 – Todd – Gut Angezogen
### (Dressed Well) (1975)
This set contains a blue cotton jacket with burgundy long sleeves and collar, and red plastic button; blue jeans with white stitching; red tricot dickey; and red vinyl oxfords.

### NRFB: $45.00

### 7972 – Todd – Zum Spielplatz
### (To the Playground) (1975)
This fashion ensemble comes with blue and white pinstriped cotton overalls; matching cap; white tricot short-sleeved top with red stitching; and red vinyl oxfords.

### NRFB: $45.00+

# Tutti & Todd Dolls' World

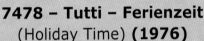

### 7974 – Todd – Pulli und Hose
### (Pullover and Pants) (1975)
This set features an olive green knit long-sleeved shirt; tan cotton slacks with green stitching; brown vinyl belt with red buckle; olive green knit short socks; and brown vinyl oxfords.
### NRFB: $35.00

### 7478 – Tutti – Ferienzeit
### (Holiday Time) (1976)
This ensemble includes a red, white, blue, and green sleeveless empire-waist dress with red bodice and lace trim, and two white plastic buttons; matching sun hat; white tricot panties with lace trim; matching slip; short white tricot socks; and white vinyl oxfords.
### NRFB: $45.00+

### 7479 – Tutti – Zum Spielplatz
### (To the Playground) (1976)
This set contains a green cotton floral long-sleeved blouse with white rickrack collar, cuffs and edging; white cotton pants; green knit ribbed skirt; and white vinyl oxfords.
### NRFB: $45.00+

### 7480 – Tutti – Grosse Ferien
### (Big Holiday) (1976)
This set includes a red, white, and blue diamond-pattern knit dress with long tricot sleeves and red cord waist tie; matching knit cap; red tricot tights; and red vinyl oxfords.
### NRFB: $45.00+

# Tutti & Todd Dolls' World

## 7481 – Tutti – Kindergeburtstag
### (Child's Birthday) (1976)

This fashion set has a red, white, blue, and yellow abstract-print sleeveless full-length dress with red tie closure; a matching head scarf; a white tricot short-sleeved blouse with red bow; and white or red bow flats.

### NRFB: $45.00+

## 7482 – Todd – Grosse Ferien
### (Big Holiday) (1976)

This grouping contains a red, blue, green, and white floral print long-sleeved shirt; red cotton shorts; a blue tricot vest; white tricot knee-high socks; and red vinyl oxfords.

### NRFB: $45.00

## 7483 – Todd – Neue Jeansmode
### (New Jean Style) (1976)

This set features a green cotton jacket with green floral bodice and sleeves with two white plastic buttons; green cotton pants; orange knit ribbed short-sleeved top; short white tricot socks; and brown vinyl oxfords.

### NRFB: $45.00

## 7484 – Todd – Huebsch zur Schule
### (Handsome for School) (1976)

This ensemble comes with a beige tricot long-sleeved shirt; red knit ribbed vest; red, white, and blue diamond-pattern knit pants; and red vinyl oxfords.

### NRFB: $45.00

# Tutti & Todd Dolls' World

## 7485 – Todd – Zum Spielplatz
### (To the Playground) (1976)

This set includes a red, white, blue, and yellow floral print cotton shirt with one white plastic button; white cotton shorts with red stitching; red tricot knee-high socks; red vinyl baseball cap; and white vinyl oxfords.

**NRFB: $35.00+**

## 9475 – Tutti – Im Kindergarten
### (In Kindergarten) (1977)

This ensemble features a yellow with white polka dot short-sleeved blouse, blue collar and red accent bow; red ribbed vest; blue skirt with center pleat and red waistband; yellow tricot panties with lace trim; yellow tricot knee-high socks; and red vinyl oxfords.

**Variation:** Shown in German dealer catalog with a yellow blouse with multicolored strawberry print.

**NRFB: $45.00+**

## 9476 – Tutti – Schnee Floeckchen
### (Snow Flakes) (1977)

This set has a red fleece coat with braid trim, two white plastic buttons, and white faux fur edging; matching hood; blue tricot tights; and red vinyl boots.

**Variation:** Shown in German dealer catalog with blue tricot scarf.

**NRFB: $45.00+**

## 9477 – Tutti – Bequem und Praktisch
### (Comfortable and Practical) (1977)

This ensemble includes a beige and red floral print short-sleeved cotton dress with red rickrack trim and beige inset bodice; matching beige and red floral panties; a red cotton apron with two pockets and white stitching; a cardboard blue "Coloring book"; and red bow flats.

**NRFB: $65.00+**

Collection of Priscilla Wardlow

# Tutti & Todd Dolls' World

## 9478 – Tutti – Festlich Angezogen
### (Dressed Festive) **(1977)**

This set features a dark pink nylon full-length sleeveless dress with white lace apron; matching lace bonnet; bouquet of flowers; and white bow flats.

### NRFB: $65.00+

## 9479 – Todd – Neue Jeansmode
### (New Jean Style) **(1977)**

This ensemble comes with a lime green jacket with yellow sleeves, collar and waistband; aqua, yellow, and white striped tricot short-sleeved top; blue jeans with white stitching; a blue cap with yellow vinyl bill; short yellow tricot socks; and white vinyl oxfords.

### NRFB: $50.00+

## 9480 – Todd – Ring Bearer (1977)

This set contains a burnt orange velveteen blazer with white stitching and two white plastic buttons; matching shorts; a satin pillow with sewn-on ring; white tricot knee-high socks; and white vinyl oxfords.

### NRFB: $125.00+

## 9481 – Todd – Karo-Mode
### (Square Style) **(1977)**

This set has a pair of green, brown, and white plaid pants; a matching cap with white visor; a red knit ribbed shirt with white tricot long sleeves and collar; a blue plastic transistor radio; and brown vinyl oxfords.

### NRFB: $45.00+

# Tutti & Todd Dolls' World

## 9482 – Todd – Warm Angezogen
### (Dressed Warm) **(1977)**

This set contains a red hooded parka with tan faux fur trim and brown leather-look pocket trim and toggles; a pair of brown cotton pants; a blue tricot sleeveless top; and brown vinyl oxfords.

**NRFB: $50.00+**

## 2184 – Tutti – Am Strand
### (On the Beach) **(1978)**

This ensemble features a yellow cotton one-sleeved halter-top with hot pink kite appliqué; matching head scarf; matching panties; matching pants; and yellow vinyl oxfords.

**NRFB: $50.00+**

## 2185 – Tutti – Gute Nacht
### (Good Night) **(1978)**

This set has hot pink and white fleece footed pajamas with two white bows; a matching blanket; and matching doll pajamas.

**NRFB: $45.00+**

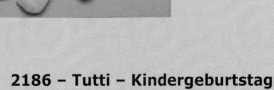

## 2186 – Tutti – Kindergeburtstag
### (Child's Birthday) **(1978)**

This set includes an aqua full-length sleeveless dress with beige lace trim; a matching sun hat with ribbon hat band; a hot pink cardboard present with green ribbon and pink flower accent; and white bow flats.

**NRFB: $65.00+**

# Tutti & Todd Dolls' World

Collection of Priscilla Wardlow

### 2187 – Tutti – Anuschka (One of a Kind) (1978)

This grouping has a beige, blue, green, and pink floral cotton empire-waist dress with large fold-over beige collar and red ribbon waistband; a red, white, and blue print cotton headscarf with red grosgrain ribbon ties; red tricot tights; a red plastic suitcase; and red vinyl oxfords.

**NRFB: $65.00+**

### 2188 – Todd – Zum Spielplatz
### (To the Playground) (1978)

This ensemble features a light blue long-sleeved cotton jacket with red large pin stripes; matching knickers; a red tricot sleeveless top; red tricot knee-high socks; and slate blue vinyl oxfords.

**NRFB: $45.00**

### 2189 – Todd – Drachensteigen
### (Flying a Kite) (1978)

This set contains aqua cotton overalls; an aqua, yellow, and white tricot short-sleeved shirt; a yellow cotton cap; an aqua, yellow, and green cardboard kite with red ribbon tail and white pull-string; and white vinyl oxfords.

**NRFB: $65.00+**

Collection of Annette Nott

Collections of Paul David and Annette Nott

# Tutti & Todd Dolls' World

Collection of Annette Nott

### 2190 – Todd – Ausflug
### (A Trip) (1978)
This set has a white cotton jumpsuit with red stitching; matching sailor hat; red cotton vest with white stitching; and white vinyl oxfords.

### NRFB: $50.00+

### 2191 – Todd – Auf Grosse Reise
### (Going on a Big Trip) (1978)
This group includes a blue velveteen long-sleeved blazer with yellow stitching and two yellow plastic buttons; matching sailor cap; yellow cotton shorts with blue stitching; yellow tricot knee-high socks; and pale yellow vinyl oxfords (may have been white at one time).

### NRFB: $45.00+

### 2650 – Tutti – Sonntagskleid
### (Sunday Dress) (1979)
This ensemble contains a full-length sundress with white bodice and skirt of Barbie doll's Quick Curl fabric; matching sun hat with black ties; matching jacket; and white vinyl oxfords.

### NRFB: $55.00+

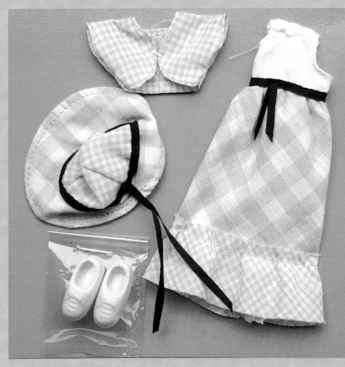

### 2651 – Tutti – Blumenmaedchen
#### (Flower Girl) **(1979)**

This set includes a white full-length sundress with splashes of yellow roses and yellow attached apron; a yellow cotton short-sleeved blouse with lace trim; and white vinyl oxfords.

#### NRFB: $45.00+

### 2652 – Tutti – Spaziergang
#### (A Walk) **(1979)**

This set features a blue fleece jacket with white fleece collar and white edging on cuffs; a light blue sleeveless dress with orange rose print and edging; white tricot knee-high socks; and white vinyl oxfords.

#### NRFB: $50.00+

### 2653 – Tutti – Spielplatz
#### (The Playground) **(1979)**

This set has a green and white checked play suit with white eyelet trim; matching pants; a white cotton crop top with green stitching and eyelet edging; and white vinyl oxfords.

#### NRFB: $50.00+

# Tutti & Todd Dolls' World

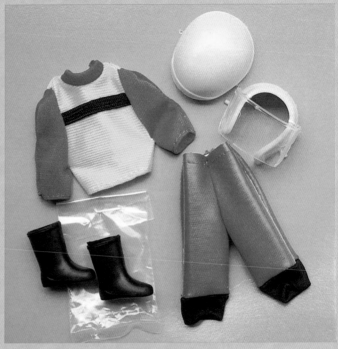

### 2654 – Todd – Vatis Helfer
(Dad's Helper) **(1979)**
This set includes a yellow nylon jacket with blue collar and trim; yellow nylon pants; a red plastic fireman's hat; a red plastic axe; and blue vinyl boots.
### NRFB: $55.00+

### 2655 – Todd – Motorcycle Rider
**(1979)**
This set has a yellow nylon long-sleeved jersey with red sleeves and black stripe on front; red vinyl pants with black elastic and ankles; a yellow plastic helmet; yellow plastic headpiece with attached clear plastic visor; and black vinyl boots.
*At the time of publishing we were not able to confirm the actual German name for this fashion.
### NRFB: $50.00+

### 2656 – Todd – Kindergarten
(Kindergarten) **(1979)**
Gold tricot long-sleeved shirt; red, orange, white and black plaid cotton slacks; a matching vest; a black tricot cap; and black vinyl oxfords.
### NRFB: $40.00+

# Tutti & Todd Dolls' World

## 2657 – Todd – Grosse Ferien
### (Big Holiday) (1979)
This set features a blue fleece pullover with hood, white ties and waistband; a white short-sleeved shirt; white slacks with brown pin stripes; and white vinyl oxfords.

**NRFB: $50.00+**

Collection of Paul David

## 8912 – Todd – Zirkusclown
### (Circus Clown) (1980)
This set includes a turquoise and yellow nylon clown's suit; matching hat; and yellow velveteen clown's floppy shoes.

**NRFB: $75.00+**

## 8913 – Todd – Schulanfang
### (School Beginning) (1980)
This group features brown and white print cotton knickers with attached suspenders with two brown plastic buttons; a gold tricot short-sleeved shirt; a brown tricot long-sleeved jacket with gold tricot collar; gold tricot knee-high socks; and brown vinyl oxfords.

**NRFB: $65.00+**

185

# Tutti & Todd Dolls' World

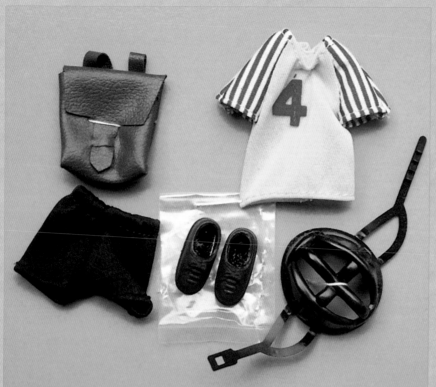

## 8914 – Todd – Sportsfreund
### (Sport Friend) (1980)
This set includes a yellow tricot shirt with blue and yellow striped sleeves and red velveteen number "4" on front; black tricot shorts; a brown vinyl backpack; a black plastic helmet; and black plastic oxfords.

**NRFB: $45.00+**

## 8915 – Todd – Cowboy (1980)
This ensemble contains a red, black, and green plaid short-sleeved cotton shirt; light blue jeans with red stitching; red tricot neck scarf; tan velveteen chaps with attached brown vinyl belt; carmel vinyl cowboy hat; and brown vinyl oxfords.

**NRFB: $95.00+**

## 8946 – Tutti – Zirkusstar
### (Circus Star) (1980)
This set contains a turquoise and yellow nylon circus costume with gold braid; a turquoise nylon cape with gold braid headband; and yellow sheer tights.

**NRFB: $75.00+**

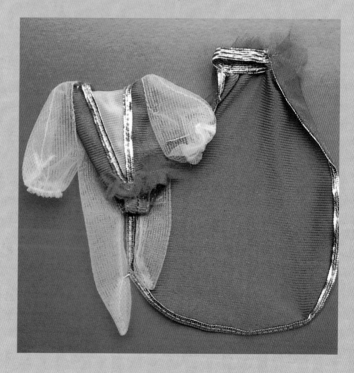

## 8947 – Tutti – Spielkleid
### (Play Dress) (1980)

This set features a red, green, and pink floral print cotton smock; a pink tricot ruffled slip; pink tricot short socks; and pale pink vinyl oxfords.

**NRFB: $45.00+**

## 8948 – Tutti – Turnerin
### (Gymnast) (1980)

This ensemble includes an orange nylon jacket with white collar; orange nylon shorts with white edging; a white tricot halter top; a white vinyl visor; short white tricot socks; and white vinyl oxfords.

**NRFB: $45.00+**

## 8949 – Tutti – Nostalgie
### (Nostalgia) (1980)

This group has a yellow tricot long-sleeved blouse with lace trim; an orange cotton vest; a black full skirt with red and yellow and green floral print and lace trim; and brown vinyl oxfords.

**NRFB: $45.00+**

# Tutti & Todd Dolls' World

## Tutti & Todd Vinyl and Licensed Products

Tutti Play
Cases
$35.00 each

Tutti & Chris Doll Case, "Balloons"
$45.00+ (HTF)

Tutti & Chris Patio
Picnic Case
$95.00

Tutti Play Case
$95.00

Tutti & Chris Doll Case
$45.00+ (HTF)

Collection of Marl Davidson

Tutti & Todd House
$45.00

Tutti Playhouse – $45.00

Tutti & Chris House
$150.00 (HTF)

# Tutti & Todd Dolls' World

**Tutti's Summer House**
**$75.00+**

Collection of Barry Sturgill

**Tutti & Chris
House-Mate
Sears Exclusive
$50.00+**

Collection of Franklin Lim Lao

Courtesy of 1975 Mattel German dealer catalog

**Barbie, Francie, Casey &
Tutti Doll Trunk by S.P.P.
©1966 – hard plastic
$100.00+ (HTF)**

**Barbie and Her Friends
Wedding Trousseau
Trunk with Tutti
$75.00+ (HTF)**

**Tutti-Koffer
(German Tutti case)
"Train No. 5" case
$100+ (VHTF)**

Collection of Sandi Holder

Collection of Shannon Bilawchuk

Courtesy of Marl Davidson

**Todd Lunch Box
"Western" scene – by
Ardee Mfg. Co.
$200.00+ (VHTF)**

**Tutti in Paris Lunch Box
by Ardee Industries
$200.00+**

**Tutti Ice Cream Stand
NRFB: $295.00+
$200.00+ (VHTF)**

**Chapter 4**

Collection of Sandi Holder

**Palmolive Soap with
Tutti Doll Premium Offer
$200.00+ (VERY RARE)**

**Tutti & Todd Dutch Bedroom Set
by Suzy Goose**
This set also has a coat rack with blue plastic Suzy Goose hangers, not shown in photo.

**NRFB – $1,000.00+
M/C: $600.00+ (VERY RARE)**

**Tutti Paper
Dolls
by Whitman
$25.00**

**Tutti Paper Dolls
by Whitman
$35.00+ (HTF)**

## Samples and Prototypes

Sample Chris doll with purple hair bow (instead of green), wearing a red floral dress. Pattern is hand painted on fabric.

Variation of 7453 – Tutti's New Swing-A-Ling/Tuttis Neue Schaukel (Tutti's New Swing) Tutti doll is holding the production version.

Courtesy of Barry Sturgill

Courtesy of Barry Sturgill

This sweet sleeveless dress is a production sample that was never produced. Note the very strange straw "hat" without a crown and irregular shaped, hand-cut brim.

Courtesy of Barry Sturgill

Collection of Judy Schizas

Top left: Sample Tutti fashion, probably for European market.

Tutti and Todd dolls wearing samples that may have been intended as a matching set. Tutti's fashion is made from the same pattern as #3603 Sand Castles, and Todd's jacket is made from Barbie's #1637 Outdoor Life.

Collection of Judy Schizas

# Chapter 5
# Skipper Doll's Pak Attack

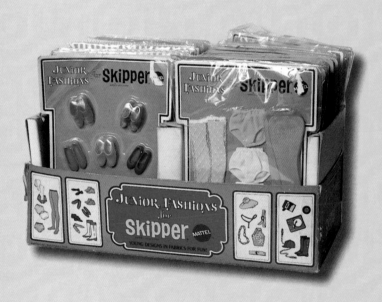

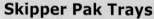

### Skipper Pak Trays

These very hard-to-find countertop display trays were available only to retailers when purchasing a certain quantity or predetermined assortment of outfits.

**$100.00+ each** (Paks not included)

# Skipper Doll's Pak Attack

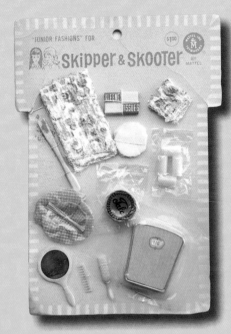

### Beauty Bath (1965 – 1966)

This group contains pink floral terrycloth towel; a matching washcloth; four pink plastic rollers; box of Kleenex tissue; pink plastic mirror, comb, and brush; pink and silver cardboard scale; blue plastic shower cap; gold cardboard talc box; orange sponge on a pink plastic handle (sponge has almost always deteriorated to nothing); and blue powder puff with blue satin handle.

### MOC: $95.00+

### Hats 'n Hats (1965 – 1966)

This group contains a straw hat with red satin hatband (Same as #1901 Red Sensation); red velvet hat (Same as #1906 Dress Coat); navy cotton duck hat with white stitching; and light pink cotton hat with lace ruffle brim (matches pak dress Party Pink).

### MOC: $50.00+

### Just for Fun (1965 – 1967)

This ensemble has red vinyl rollerskates with gray plastic wheels; white vinyl ice skates with gray plastic blades; wooden bat; plastic baseball; red and white jump rope with black handles; red wooden yo-yo; miniature "Barbie" doll; and red and white checked cotton skirt for the "Barbie" doll.

### MOC: $125.00+

### Party Pink (1965 – 1967)

This features a pink cotton sleeveless dress with sheer lace overskirt and shoulder straps (this is identical to the dress from #1904 Flower Girl except for color).

### MOC: $45.00+
### M/C: $25.00 – 30.00

# Skipper Doll's Pak Attack

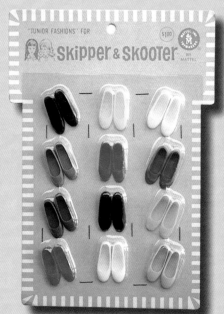

### Shoe Parade (1965 – 1966)
This group contains 12 pairs of flats: double pairs of black, white, and red; single pairs of royal blue, yellow, turquoise, green, pink, and light blue.

### MOC: $60.00+

### Wooly PJ's (1965 – 1967)
This set contains red flannel pajamas with yellow flower print and fringe trim, and a yellow plastic brush.

### MOC: $50.00
### M/C: $20.00 – 25.00

### Happy Times (1970)
This set has a hot pink and blue plastic record player; red label "Barbie" record; turquoise knee-high boots; red and white jump rope; turquoise vinyl riding hat; yellow English book; green Arithmetic book; black vinyl book strap; and two pencils in red and tan.

### MOC: $75.00

### Nighty Nice (1970)
This ensemble contains aqua cotton shorty pajamas with white polka dots and lace trim; an aqua plastic princess phone; cardboard face mirror; and yellow scuffs with yellow tricot accents.

### MOC: $35.00+; M/C: $25.00

# Skipper Doll's Pak Attack

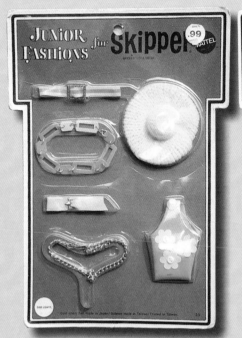  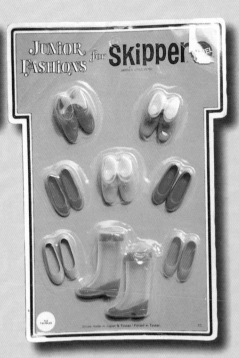

### Side Lights (1970)

This group has a yellow knit tam hat; hot pink vinyl purse with three yellow flowers (same as purse from #1738 Fancy Pants); yellow vinyl belt with gold buckle; hot pink plastic chain belt (same as belt from #1961 Real Sporty); yellow and pink striped vinyl belt with gold buckle; and gold chain belt.

### MOC: $75.00+; M/C: $40.00+

### Summer Slacks (1970)

This group contains a one-piece jumpsuit with two belt loops (top is knit, bottoms are denim or cotton); a yellow vinyl belt; and rose sunglasses (this has been found in numerous colors and fabrics).

### MOC: $45.00+
### M/C: $15.00 – 30.00
### depending on unusual or HTF fabric variations

### Toe Twinkles (1970)

This set has three pairs of vinyl ankle boots: green, red, and hot pink; four pairs of flats: red, royal blue, turquoise, and pink; and one pair of clear vinyl rain boots with red trim.

### MOC: $45.00+

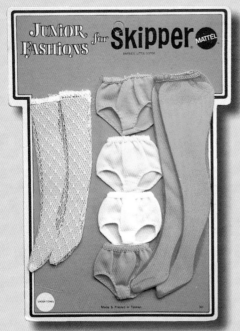

### Undertones (1970)

This set contains four tricot panties in yellow, white, coral, and hot pink; and two pair of tights, pantyhose, or stockings in varied styles and colors.

**MOC: $45.00+**

### Skimmer 'n Scarf (1971)

This set contains a sleeveless dress with empire waist accented by hot pink ribbon and matching head scarf (fabrics are lime, orange, white, gold and pink abstract, geometric print, or pink floral used for Tutti doll's #3617 Birthday Beauties).

**MOC: $45.00; M/C: $25.00 – 35.00**

### Check the Slacks (1971)

In this group are bell-bottom pants with scalloped waist and two yellow buttons; and black flats. These pants came in a variety of fabrics and colors.

**MOC: $45.00; M/C: $20.00 – 30.00**

### Action Fashion (1971)

This ensemble contains red flats; white ice skates with gray plastic blades; yellow vinyl galoshes; a red and white jump rope with clear handles; white plastic ball; yellow plastic transistor radio; and lavender sunglasses.

**MOC: $75.00+**

# Skipper Doll's Pak Attack

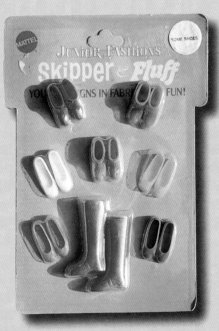

### The Slumber Party (1971)
This set has a flannel robe with white cord tie and lace trim (fabrics are red, and shades of pink or light blue with polka dots or stripes).

**MOC: $35.00; M/C: $15.00 – 20.00**

### Sporty Shorty (1971)
This group has a sleeveless cotton crop top with ruffle; a matching full miniskirt; and orange flats (fabrics are royal blue with white polka dots, or orange, pink, and white striped fabric from #1960 Trim Twosome).

**MOC: $35.00+**

### Some Shoes (1971)
This ensemble contains three pairs of ankle boots: red, green, and hot pink; red knee-high boots; and four pairs of flats: white, yellow, orange, and royal blue.
*This Pak is HTF still on the card.*

**MOC: $50.00+**

# Chapter 6
# Gift Sets

For many collectors, gift sets are the holy grail of collecting. They usually contain multiple outfits and accessories, many of them unique to the specific gift set, have spectacular graphics, and were the most expensive items (and therefore the most coveted by children) being sold in the line. Many of them were specific to a single department store, Sears and Roebuck.

When pricing or buying these, it's important to remember that all gift sets are difficult to find. However, most sets included dolls and/or ensembles that were available as part of the regular line. These items do not have a different value than when they are found loose and in mint condition. Therefore, the price of a gift set reflects not only its rarity, but the uniqueness of its specific outfits and/or accessories contained in the set. It's only when all the pieces (whether regular line or not) are combined with their original packaging that they command top value.

For gift sets, NRFB condition means that dolls have their original outfit (when applicable), head cellos (when applicable), stands, fashion booklets, and wrist tags. Fashions should have their original cello, and clothing and accessories should be sewn to the original liner or in attached cello bags. The box itself should be in factory-perfect condition without dents, scratches, split corners, tears, or water stains. A MIB gift set would be in the identical condition of one that is NRFB, but the contents would be removed from the original card and cello and cello bags may be missing or removed. The doll's original wrist tag and head wrap may or may not be attached. Missing or less-than-mint pieces to gift sets, damaged or repaired boxes, and/or missing box liners substantially lower the market value.

## 1021 – Skipper Party Time Gift Set (1965 – 1966)

The first Skipper gift set to be issued by Mattel, this gift set followed the established Barbie trend by including outfits already available. The Skipper Party Time Gift Set came with a straight-leg Skipper doll wearing her red and white swimsuit. Additionally, Silk 'n Fancy (stock #1902) and Dress Coat (stock #1906) were included in the set. Silk 'n Fancy, a white satin dress with red velvet bodice, came with a gold elastic stretch headband. Dress Coat, a red velvet coat with gold bead buttons, came with a matching red velvet purse and hat. One pair of socks, short white gloves, and white flats were included for completion of both ensembles. The gift set was issued again the following year and was titled Skipper and Her Friend Skooter Party Time Set, and the new box description adds "Costumes fit Skooter."

**NRFB: $450.00 – 500.00**
**MIB: $295.00+**

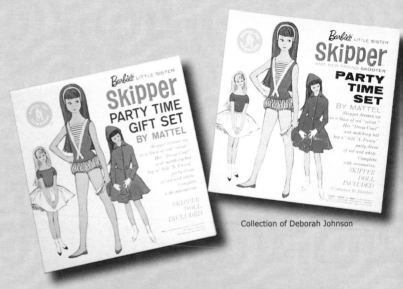

Collection of Deborah Johnson

# Gift Sets

### 1032 – Skipper on Wheels (1965)

This gift set included pieces from existing ensembles as well as extra accessories that could not be purchased elsewhere. This set included the white "Barbie" print bodysuit and red skirt with matching "Barbie" print pocket from Day at the Fair (stock #1911) as well as the navy cotton pants, embroidered navy blouse, and navy jacket with lime green accents from Fun Time (stock #1920). Additionally this set came with a red wooden yo-yo, red plastic glasses, red plastic rollerskates with silver plastic "wheels," a pair of royal blue flats, and a pair of red flats. Exclusive to the set were a red plastic skateboard with yellow trim, red plastic scooter with "Skipper" printed on it in yellow, and a red cotton boating hat. This set did not come with a doll.

**NRFB: $450.00 – 500.00**
**MIB: $395.00+**

### 1036 – Skooter with her Cut 'n Button Costumes (1965 – 1967)

Skooter doll's first and only gift set was issued in 1965 with items exclusive to the set. In the style of the "Sew-Free" fashions, there were three outfits for Skooter doll that could be cut out and "sewn" together by the child. An adorable pink nightgown with floral print, matching night cap, and pink fabric scuffs, a red coat with navy blue trim and blue vinyl belt with gold buckle, and a sweet blue gingham sundress with ship decals and red flats were included. The outfits came with special directions and Sew-Free strips showing the child where and how to cut the outfits in order to create fun ensembles for Skooter doll "without sewing a stitch!" This set came with a straight-leg Skooter doll in either brunette, blonde, or titian dressed in her red and white swimsuit.
*This gift set is HTF.*

**NRFB: $350.00 – 400.00**
**MIB: $250.00+**

### 1039 – Skipper Holiday Party Set (1965)

This gift set included the same clothing as Skipper Party Time Gift Set; however, the outfits are packaged on a larger cardboard insert to fit the larger box format.  The doll included with this set is the bendable leg Skipper in her pink "bendable leg" box liner.  Image shown to left. Either the tan or pink skinned bendable leg doll were included. A paper label was attached to the box end to note which hair color was included.
*This gift set is VERY RARE.*

**NRFB: $895.00+; MIB: $695.00+**

201

# Gift Sets

## Sears' Own Skipper & Skooter Gift Set (1967)

Offered exclusively through the Sears catalog, this set featured a Skipper & Skooter vinyl case complete with Beachy Peachy (stock #1938) and All Prettied Up (stock #1949), Cello wrapped together and stapled on the inside lid of the case. A pink-skinned, bendable-leg Skipper and a pink-skinned, bendable-leg Skooter in their original bathing suits were also included.

The only information about this set is from the original Sears catalog picture and description. There is no stock number listed, and it's unclear whether the dolls had wrist tags or not. This set has no added value if just pieced together – it must have outfits on the card, intact with cellophane to be considered "Sears' Own Skipper and Skooter Gift Set."

*This gift set is extremely rare* — it is the only known example we have found.

### NRFB: $750.00+

Courtesy of *Barbie Bazaar*

Collection of Cheryl Nelson

## 1546 – Skipper Perfectly Pretty Set (Sears Exclusive) (1968)

This gift set came with a beautiful 1968 TNT Skipper doll dressed in her turquoise and pink swimsuit. An exclusive outfit was included: a turquoise velvet dropped waist dress with white cotton ruffled bodice and hot pink ribbon belt, a turquoise velvet empire waist coat with vinyl belt with gold buckle, and a matching turquoise velvet hat with grosgrain ribbon ties. Turquoise flats completed the ensemble.

*This gift set is VHTF.*

### NRFB: $700.00 – 750.00; MIB: $400.00 – 500.00

# Gift Sets

## 1590 – Skipper Bright 'n Breezy Set (Sears Exclusive) (1969)

This elusive gift set offered by Sears came with a sausage curl TNT Skipper doll, dressed in her orange and pink swimsuit, and an exclusive outfit. This groovy ensemble consisted of a turquoise knit culotte with green yarn trim and a green "leather" bow at the waist. A matching green "leather" coat had blue "fur" trim. Green flats completed the outfit.

Collectors often refer to this gift set as "Wow! What A Cool Outfit," because it was so titled in the Sears catalog. We have been unable to confirm that the outfit was also produced and available separately with this name.
*This gift set is RARE.*

### NRFB: $750.00 – 800.00
### MIB: $500.00 – 600.00

Collection of Marcie Melillo

## 1586 – Dramatic New Living Skipper Very Best Velvet Set (Sears Exclusive) (1970 – 1971)

This gift set came with a beautiful pale blonde Dramatic New Living Skipper doll, dressed in her blue, green, and hot pink swimsuit, and an exclusive outfit. This outfit is very similar to the Perfectly Pretty Set offered just two years before. This set included an orange velvet dress with yellow organdy flounce, orange stitched trim, and a blue ribbon waistband. An orange velvet coat with yellow satin lining, attached yellow and orange plastic belt with two gold bead button closures, sheer yellow pantyhose, and yellow flats completed the ensemble.
*This gift set is VHTF.*

### NRFB: $600.00 – 700.00
### MIB: $400.00 – 500.00

# Gift Sets

Collection of Carmen Tickal

## 1249 – Living Fluff Sunshine Special (Sears Exclusive) (1971)

Fluff doll's exclusive gift set came with a Living Fluff doll dressed in her yellow, orange, and green ribbed swimsuit with orange vinyl "skirt" and her yellow plastic skateboard. Several unique outfit pieces could be coordinated to create different fun looks. This set came with a pair of red velveteen pants with yellow and blue rickrack trim, a knee-length, tricot, "gypsy-print" ruffled skirt, a matching head scarf, a white cotton peasant blouse with yellow, blue, and red rickrack trim, and a gold velveteen vest with red rick racktrim. Gold opaque tights and gold flats exclusive to the set completed the ensemble. Although this gift set was designed exclusively for Fluff doll, the fashion is tagged "Skipper."
*This gift set is VHTF.*

### NRFB: $350.00 – 400.00; MIB: $250.00+

## 1179 – Pose 'n Play Skipper and Her Swing-A-Rounder Gym (1972 – 1973)

This unique gift set was interesting in that it came with an exclusive play accessory rather than an outfit. Offered in 1972 and 1973, this set came with the Pose 'n Play Skipper doll, available only in this set this year. An orange, pink, green, and yellow plastic "gym" was included, offering "four kinds of playground fun!" The catalog description says "sturdy gym features slide-down-around pole, a trapeze for tricks, double glider, single swing." Mattel went on to explain that "Skipper doll's new "swinging-free" arms let her play on the trapeze "like a real little girl." "She can hang down, swing all the way 'round! Her waist, head, elbows and legs are very poseable, too!"
*This gift set is HTF.*

### NRFB: $150.00 – 200.00+; MIB: $100.00+

# Chapter 7
# Skipper Cases, Trunks & Vinyl Products

# Skipper Cases, Trunks & Vinyl Products

**Skipper & Skooter "Portraits" Rectangular Doll Case (vinyl) – by SPP ©1965**
**$30.00 – 40.00 each**

**Skipper & Skooter "Portraits" Train Case (vinyl) – by SPP ©1965 RARE**
**$75.00 – 100.00**

**Skipper & Skooter "Portraits" Round Hat Box (vinyl) - by SPP ©1965 – HTF**
**$50.00 – 75.00 each**

**Skipper Small Hat Box (vinyl)**
**Skipper wearing School Days, Red Sensation, and Dress Coat**
**by SPP ©1965**
**Sold in Canada**
**$75.00+**

**Skipper Small Hat Box Skipper wearing Silk 'n Fancy; Barbie wearing Silken Flame; and Ken wearing Tuxedo**
**by SPP ©1964**
**$125.00+**

# Skipper Cases, Trunks & Vinyl Products

Skipper & Skooter
"Running on the Beach"
Doll Case (vinyl)
by Mattel
HTF – $45.00 – 60.00

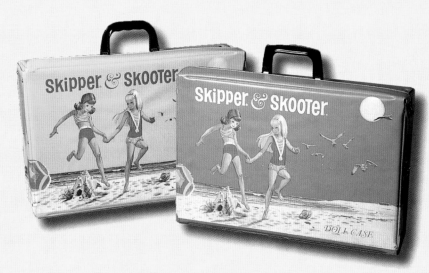

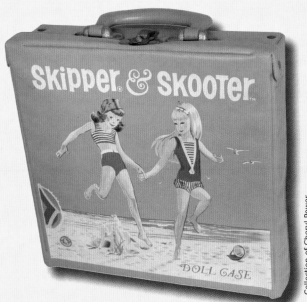

Collection of Cheryl Power

Skipper & Skooter "Running on the Beach"
Doll Case (vinyl), 10½" square
Made in Australia
by Mattel S.A. International
VHTF – $150.00+

Skipper Carrying Case (vinyl)
Wearing School Days, Red
Sensation, and Dress Coat
by SPP ©1964
$25.00 – 30.00

# Skipper Cases, Trunks & Vinyl Products

Skipper wearing Dress Coat, "At the Airport"
Small Hatbox (vinyl) – by SPP
RARE - $150.00+

Matching "Skipper" logo Train Case (vinyl)
by SPP
RARE – yellow case shows illustration on back
$150.00+

©Barbie Bazaar

Barbie and Skipper Vanity Trunk (vinyl)
by Mattel ©1965
RARE - $250.00+

Skipper & Skooter Doll Case – Skipper wearing
Fun Time or Skipper wearing School Girl  (vinyl) –
Made in France by Mattel S.A. International.  Each
case was available in either blue or yellow.
VHTF – $75.00+

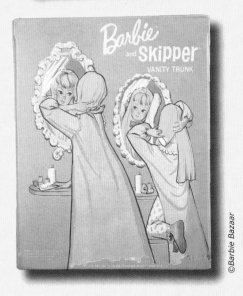

©Barbie Bazaar

Skipper & Skooter Doll Wardrobe Mallette Garde-
Robe –Black vinyl rectangular case with head
shots of Skipper and Skooter.  Made in France.
HTF – $75.00+

Skipper Small Hatbox – Black vinyl case with 8½"
circumference.  Skipper is wearing "Dreamtime."
Made in France, Mattel S.A. International.
HTF – $75.00+

# Skipper Cases, Trunks & Vinyl Products

**Skipper wearing Land and Sea "Sailing" Doll Case
(vinyl) – by Mattel
HTF – $45.00 – 60.00**
Sold in the U.S. in the 1960s, as well as in Europe
in the 1970s.

**Skooter wearing Country Picnic Doll Case (vinyl)
by Mattel ©1965
HTF – $75.00+**

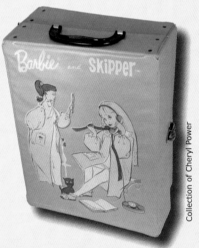

Collection of Cheryl Power

**Skipper & Barbie Trunk
Barbie wearing Nighty
Negligee, Skipper wearing
Dreamtime. ©1964
Case sold in Canada
HTF – $125.00+**

Collection of Priscilla Wardlow

**Skooter Wearing Platter
Party and Sunny Pastels
Doll Case – by Mattel
©1965
RARE – $75.00+**

Chapter 7

# Skipper Cases, Trunks & Vinyl Products

Skipper wearing Fun Time with Barbie and Ken "At a Picnic" Travel Trunk (vinyl) (left); by SPP ©1965
HTF – $75.00+

Skipper wearing Ship Ahoy! with Barbie and Francie "European Travel" Doll Trunk (vinyl) (right)  by SPP©1965
HTF – $75.00+

**Barbie & Skipper – Skipper wearing Red Sensation and Barbie wearing Sheath Sensation Carrying Case (vinyl) – by SPP ©1965**
**$35.00+**

This trunk was produced in blue or beige, and came with a clear vinyl zippered garment bag with metal hook. Bag should be inside the trunk to be considered complete.

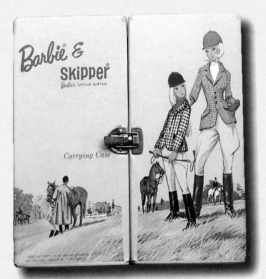

**Barbie & Skipper "Equestrienne" Carrying Case (vinyl) – by SPP ©1964**
**VHTF – $100.00+**

This trunk, also available in turquoise, came with a clear vinyl zippered garment bag with metal hook, and should be inside the trunk to be considered complete.

# Skipper Cases, Trunks & Vinyl Products

**Skipper and Skooter "Pink Polka Dot" Window Doll Case (vinyl) – by SPP ©1965**
**HTF – $150.00+**

**Skipper Mod Cases:**
**(left) Skipper wearing Budding Beauty Mod Doll Case (vinyl) – by Mattel ©1969**
**Stock #4966 – $10.00 – 30.00;**
**(right) Skipper wearing Budding Beauty and Fluff Mod Doll Case (vinyl) by Mattel**
**Canada ©1970 – Stock #4966 – $30.00 – 40.00**
(Orange color variation also shown)

# Skipper Cases, Trunks & Vinyl Products

"Wedding" Barbie Trousseau Trunk with Skipper
wearing Flower Girl (hard plastic) by SPP ©1966
HTF – $100.00+

Barbie and Her
Friends Travel Trunk
(hard plastic)
RARE – $125.00+

Barbie, Stacey, Francie and Skipper wearing Posy
Party Doll Trunk
(hard plastic)
HTF – $75.00+

Collection of Cheryl Power

Skipper Pencil Case
Skipper wearing outdoor casuals, Skooter
wearing Funtime. Both girls wearing
skates – by SPP ©1965
VHTF – $200.00+

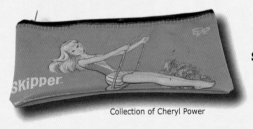

Collection of Cheryl Power

Skipper Pencil Case
Skipper wearing red and white bathing
suit, swinging. Case has zippered closure
by SPP ©1965
VHTF – $200.00+

# Skipper Cases, Trunks & Vinyl Products

**Purse-Pal (vinyl) – by SPP**
**RARE – $150.00+**

**Skipper wearing School Days,**
**Dress Coat, and Red Sensation**
**Ballet Box (vinyl)**
**by Mattel ©1964**
**VERY RARE – $200.00+**

**Skipper wearing**
**Masquerade Wallet**
**(vinyl) – by SPP ©1964**
**HTF – $45.00 – 65.00**

# Skipper Cases, Trunks & Vinyl Products

©Barbie Bazaar

**Skipper wearing Masquerade Three-Ring Binder (vinyl) by SPP ©1965**
(Also produced in yellow)
**VERY RARE – $250.00+**

**Barbie and Skipper wearing School Days Three-Ring Binder (vinyl) – by SPP**
**VHTF – $150.00+**

**Skipper Vinyl Lunch Boxes: (left) – Skipper wearing Silk 'n Fancy; (right) – Skipper wearing Country Picnic – by Mattel ©1965**
**HTF – $125.00+ each**

**Skipper Vinyl Lunch Box – by Ardee Industries: Salmon Pink Lunch Box with words "Ardee & Company presents Swan Lake A Dance Fantasy" on front of box. Year of production unknown.**
**HTF – $80.00+**

**Skipper Vinyl Lunch Box Skipper wearing School Days, Red Sensation, and Dress Coat ©1965**
**VHTF – $150.00+**

Collection of Cheryl Power          Collection of Cheryl Power

**Skipper Book Bag (vinyl) – Skipper wearing Red Sensation (left), Dress Coat (center), and School Days (right) ©1965**
**HTF – $200.00+**

# Skipper Cases, Trunks & Vinyl Products

**Skipper Coin Purse (vinyl)**
**by SPP ©1964**
**VERY RARE – $150.00 each**

**Skipper Coin Purse with Chain**
**(vinyl) – by SPP**
**VERY RARE – $150.00**

Collection of Sandi Holder

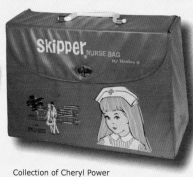

Collection of Cheryl Power

**Skipper Nurse Bag – by Hasbro®**
**Red Vinyl, Bottom stamped**
**"Hassenfeld Bros (Canada)**
**Limited**
**Montreal Canada 1785."**
**This case is 12" in width at**
**bottom and 11" at top.**
**RARE – $350.00+**

**Skipper Nurse Bag (vinyl)**
**VERY RARE – $300.00**

Collection of Leslie Bote

**Barbie, Ken & Skipper "Dove"**
**Doll Case – Medium blue vinyl,**
**Skipper wearing Red Sensation,**
**Barbie wearing Sheath**
**Sensation, and Ken wearing Best**
**Man, by Mattel ©1964**
**RARE – $150.00+**

**Skipper wearing Red Sensation,**
**"Dove" Doll Case – by Mattel**
**©1964**
**This case has been found in light**
**blue and white patent leather.**
**RARE – $150.00+**

# Chapter 8
# Licensed Products

# Licensed Products

Through the years there have been a variety of products that were made using the Skipper doll image. Ranging from coloring books to records and doll-sized furniture, these items helped the child construct a broader world in which Skipper doll and her friends could exist. Because Mattel had to approve any item using the likeness of Skipper doll or a friend, collectors today can get a clear picture of how Mattel perceived Skipper's image and what kinds of merchandise the company felt were appropriate for children to play with.

Many of the small companies that created licensed products no longer exist. These products were not manufactured in the large quantities that the dolls and outfits were, making them more difficult to find today. Because they were not part of the regular Barbie doll line, they are not shown in Mattel dealer catalogs, which adds frustration when trying to determine how the pieces were originally packaged. The values quoted in this chapter are for the items as shown. Values will fluctuate depending on condition, complete contents, and original packaging.

© Barbie Bazaar

**"The Musical World Of Barbie" – 33⅓ R.P.M. Records
by Columbia Special Products ©1965
RARE – $150.00+
The World of Barbie record – note Skipper doll is on cover.**

# Licensed Products

"A Picnic for Skipper" Record

"Skipper, Skooter and Ricky" Record
Note Skooter is wearing Ricky's shirt.

"A Happy Barbie Birthday" record –
Note the RARE blue hair ribbon in Skipper doll's hair.
RARE – $150.00+ each

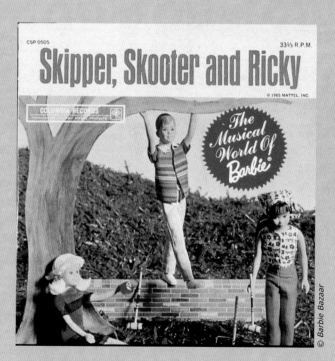

# Licensed Products

**Skipper Billfold
(cardboard)
VERY RARE – $75.00+**

**Skipper Fashion Embroidery
Set – by Standard Toycraft
©1965 – Stock #5301
RARE – $200.00+**

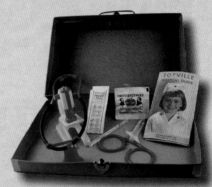

**Skipper Nurse Kit
by Hasbro
Cardboard box comes
complete with a
microscope, glasses,
syringe, stethoscope,
cough drops, Toyville
Hospital Guide, and
"microfilm."
RARE – $175.00+**

**Skipper Wrist Watch
by Bradley Co. ©1965
VERY RARE – $450.00+**

**Skipper Magic Slate
Paper Saver – by
Whitman 1964 –
Stock #4440
HTF – $50.00+**

# Licensed Products

©Barbie Bazaar

**Beach Buggy for Skipper**
**by Irwin ©1964**
**RARE – $500.00+**

## Skipper Doll's Sports Car – AKA: Allan's New Roadster – by Irwin

This car was advertised in the Montgomery Ward's 1965 catalog as "Skipper Doll's Sports Car," and is known today among collectors as "The Skipper Car." However, the original packaging (not shown) reveals that the car does not belong to Skipper, but actually to Allan, Ken's best friend. The original packaging says "Skipper rides with you in Allan's New Roadster." Perhaps since this car is smaller in design and the original identifying packaging is usually missing, collectors quickly assume this is Skipper doll's car. This car has been found in hunter green and aqua blue.

### NRFB: $250.00+; M/C: $150.00+

Collection of James Taylor

Collection of Cheryl Power

# Licensed Products

*Happy-Go-Lucky Skipper* book
by Carl Memling – Published by
Random House – ©1965
$30.00 – 40.00

Skipper Halloween Costume
by Collegeville Costumes ©1964
VHTF – $250.00+

"Skipper says 'Happy Birthday!'"
Wrapping Paper – by Whitman
RARE – $150.00+
per sheet

Skipper Linen Closet – by Merry Mfg. Co.
©1964 – Stock #2002:100
RARE – $150.00+

Skipper Party Closet – by Merry Mfg. Co.
©1964 – Stock #2001:100
RARE – $150.00+

*Not Pictured
Skipper Bath Closet – by Merry Mfg. Co.
©1964
RARE – $150.00+

# Licensed Products

Collection of Vicky Scherck

Collection of Vicky Scherck

**Skipper's Spelling Board – by Bar Zim Mfg. – one side has wooden blocks with lowercase letters; the other side has uppercase letters and a wipe-away board**
**VERY RARE – $300.00+**

**Skipper Chalk Board**
**A Product of Bar-Zim**
**Jersey City, NJ, ©1965.**
**Measures 24" X 16" and is**
**made of particle board.**
**VERY RARE – $250.00+**

Collection of Cheryl Power

**Skipper Tea Set – No known boxed examples of this set exists, so authors assume this came in a boxed set of six and the pieces are as shown.**
**HTF – $75.00+**

# Licensed Products

**Skipper Electric Drawing Set**
**by Lakeside Lifetime Toys ©1964**
**HTF – NRFB: $125.00+; M/C: $50.00+**

**Skipper Vanity Purse**
**RARE – $200.00+**

Collection of Lisa Mainetti

**Skipper Patterns – by McCall's**
**$30.00+ (uncut)**

**Page from vintage *McCall's* magazine shows early**
**Skipper Fashions made from patterns.**

Collection of Barb Roberts

# Licensed Products

Skipper's Jeweled Vanity
by Suzy Goose ©1965
Stock #414
RARE – $275.00+

Skipper's Jeweled Wardrobe
by Suzy Goose ©1965
Stock #418
RARE – $275.00+

Skipper's Jeweled Bed
by Suzy Goose ©1965
Stock #410
HTF – $250.00+

## Licensed Products

*Skipper Barbie's Little Sister* Coloring Book by Whitman ©1965 $35.00

*Barbie and Her Little Sister Skipper* Coloring Book by Whitman ©1965 $35.00

*Portrait of Skipper* Book by Mattel ©1964 $10.00

Skipper *Off to Camp Sticker Fun* by Whitman ©1965 HTF $35.00 – 50.00

Skipper Coloring Books by Whitman $15.00 – 20.00 each

## Whitman Products

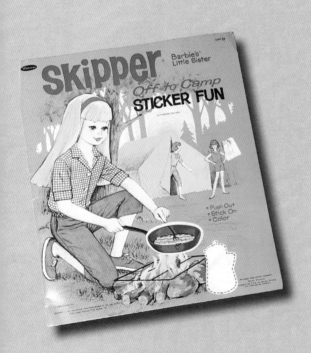

# Licensed Products

**Skipper's Day-by-Day Wardrobe Paper Doll – by Whitman ©1964**
**RARE – $195.00+**

**Skipper's Fashion Calendar Wardrobe Paper Doll – by Whitman ©1965**
**RARE – $195.00+**

**Skooter-Fashion-Go-Round Paper Doll – by Whitman ©1965 – Stock #4639**
**RARE – $195.00+**

**Skooter Paper Dolls, "3 Skooter Dolls" – by Whitman ©1965 – Stock #1985**
**VERY RARE – $225.00+**

# Licensed Products

**Skipper Paper Doll "Seahorse"**
**by Whitman ©1965**
**HTF – $40.00 – 50.00**

**Skipper and Skooter Four Seasons**
**Wardrobe Paper Dolls by Whitman ©1965**
**RARE – $195.00+**

**Skipper Paper Doll Fashions – "Pose 'n**
**Play" by Whitman ©1973 – Stock #1969**
**$15.00**

**Barbie and Skipper Paper Doll**
**by Whitman ©1964 – Stock #1957**
**$40.00 – 50.00**

**Barbie, Skipper, Skooter Paper Doll**
**by Whitman ©1966 – Stock #1976**
**$40.00 – 50.00**

Collection of Cheryl Power

# Licensed Products

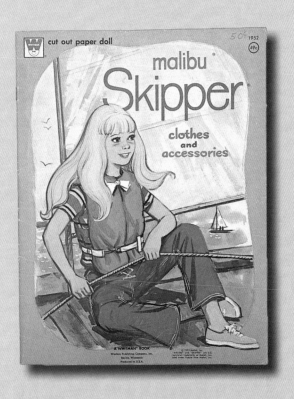

Malibu Skipper Paper doll – by Whitman
©1973 – Stock #1952
$15.00

Barbie and Skipper Frame-Tray Puzzle
"Equestrienne" – by Whitman
©1972 – Stock #4508
$35.00+

Skipper wearing School Days Frame-Tray
Puzzle – by Whitman ©1965 – Stock #4427
HTF – $60.00+

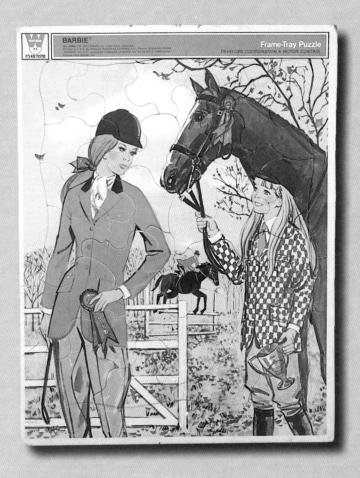

# Licensed Products

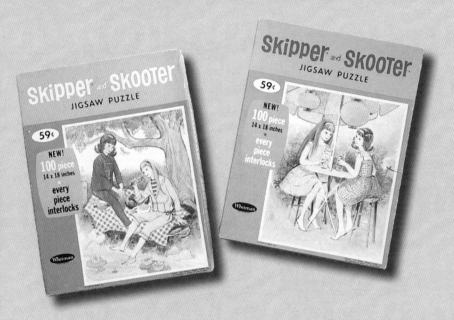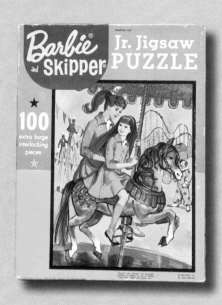

**Skipper and Skooter Jigsaw Puzzle, "Picnic Scene" – by Whitman ©1965**
**Stock #4646 – $40.00 – 50.00**

**Skipper and Skooter Jigsaw Puzzle, "Ice Cream Scene" – by Whitman ©1965**
**Stock #4646 – $40.00 – 50.00**

**Barbie and Skipper Jr. Jigsaw Puzzle "Merry-Go-Round Scene"**
**by Whitman ©1964 – Stock #4611 – $40.00 – 50.00**

*Barbie: The Mattel Barbie Magazine* **– by Mattel**
**Several issues showcasing Skipper doll**
**$15.00 – 25.00**

Chapter 8

## Barbie and Skipper School – by Mattel
### ©1965
### RARE – $500.00+

Of all structures in Barbie doll land this is probably one of the most difficult to find, and when it is found it is usually tattered and torn and is missing pieces. The six-sided structure folds out to form a complete school that includes a playground.

Contents:

Schoolroom —
Teacher's desk
Teacher's chair
Teacher's desk blotter
Teacher's vase of flowers (two pieces)
Four students' desks with attached chairs
Green painting easel
Three large paintings (houses, flowers, and covered
   wagon)
Six small paintings
World globe (two pieces)
United States flag with base
Blue wastebasket
Seven books (English, History, Civics, Reading, New Math,
   Geography, Spanish Made Easy)

Playground —
Slide (three pieces)
See-saw (two pieces)
Swing and string
Green bench
Hopscotch game
Blue outdoor trash bin with swinging lid

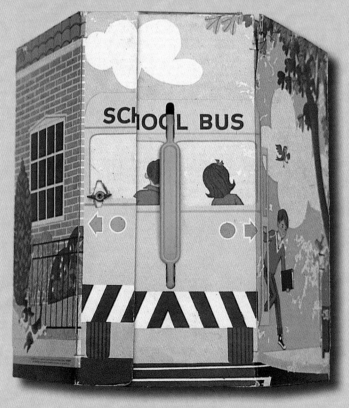

# Licensed Products

## Barbie and Skipper School, open views with contents

# Licensed Products

## Skipper Game – by Mattel ©1964
## $50.00 – 75.00

Contents:
Gameboard
Four Skipper markers (blue, yellow, orange, and red)
One small die
Four "Club Pin" picture cards (worth 20 points)
Four "Prince" picture cards (worth $25.00 and 25 points)
Four "Riding Habit" picture cards (worth $15.00)
Four "Tack" picture cards (worth $20.00)
Point cards (25, 10, and 5)
Barbie & Skipper Play Money

## Skipper 'n Skooter Go-Together Furniture Double Bunk Beds and Ladder – by Mattel ©1965
## NRFB: $195.00+; M/C: $95.00

Contents:
Yellow plastic set of bunk beds
Yellow plastic ladder
Two cardboard mattresses
Two thin paper "sew free"-style bedspreads
Two thin paper "sew free"-style pillows with foam stuffing
Yellow rug
Cardboard backdrop

©Barbie Bazaar

## Barbie 'n Skipper Go-Together Dining Room Furniture – by Mattel ©1965
## NRFB: $250.00+
## M/C: $150.00

## Barbie 'n Skipper Go-Together Living Room Furniture Group
## by Mattel ©1965
## NRFB: $150.00+
## M/C: $75.00

©Barbie Bazaar

# Licensed Products

## Skipper Dream Room
### by Mattel ©1964
### NRFB: $500.00+
### M/C: $350.00

Collection of Janet Lewis

Contents:

Main structure which can be reconfigured into many different interior and exterior floorplans
White wooden curtain rod
Two Sew-Free curtains; white dotted Swiss with turquoise trim, attached to rod with six turquoise Sew-Free buttons per curtain
Two turquoise Sew-Free curtain tiebacks
Pink cardboard floorboard for alcove
Two-piece table with "The Skipper Game" printed on top
Two cardboard, heart-backed side chairs
Cardboard study desk with two book shelves (three pieces)
Purple cardboard desk blotter
Blue cardboard telephone (one piece)
Purple cardboard lamp with yellow cardboard shade (three pieces)
Cardboard club chair (one piece)
Red wastebasket (one piece)
Green television
Blue phonograph
Records (eight)
Rectangular "cat" picture
Barbie magazines (three)
Purple framed photo of Barbie
Miniature "Barbie" Dreamhouse (three pieces)
"Talking Tatters" doll
Oval pedestal table (two pieces) held together with a bird cage
Four oval wall pictures
Turquoise oval paper fringed rug
Bed and mattress cover (two pieces)
Four Sew-Free dotted Swiss bed ruffle pieces
Yellow Sew-Free bedspread with four turquoise Sew-Free buttons
Cardboard bolster with Sew-Free cover and three Sew-Free turquoise buttons
Six Sew-Free cushions with foam inserts: one heart, one triangle, one rectangle, one octagon, and two round
Two-piece vanity with Sew-Free cushion and dotted Swiss ruffle
Two garden benches
Sew-Free stickers to apply to desk, blotter, etc.: Eight large and four small red hearts, four large and four small lavender hearts, and four large and four small yellow hearts
Eight red plastic hangers
Instruction booklet

Collection of Marl Davidson

# Licensed Products

## 9282 Growing Up Skipper 2-in-1 Bedroom
### (1976 – 1977)

Same as 1975 set not shown, but no doll included. Box graphics indicate the set is
for Skipper and new friend Growing Up Ginger.

### NRFB: $100.00+; M/C: $50.00

Collection of Franklin Lim Lao

## *Not pictured*
## 9652 Growing Up Skipper & Her 2-in-1 Bedroom (1975)

Two rooms in one – for twice as much fun! This VHTF structure (but not very desirable) for Skipper was designed to change from a cute 'little girl' bedroom into a perfect place for teenagers!" This version was probably a department store catalog item as there are no color graphics. It included a Growing Up Skipper doll; bunk beds; three bedspreads; two reversible pillows; canopy with ruffle; desk lamp; hanging lamp fixture; two books; clipboard; reversible picture; growth chart; desk with vanity storage area; mirror; chair; ladder; powder can; brush; comb; hand mirror; hardboard walls with connectors; and assorted decals.

### NRFB: $100.00+; M/C: $50.00

## 9682 Growing Up Skipper & Her 2-in-1 Bedroom (1976–1977)

Same as above, but no doll included. Box graphics indicate the set is for Skipper and new friend Growing Up Ginger.

### NRFB: $100.00+; M/C: $50.00

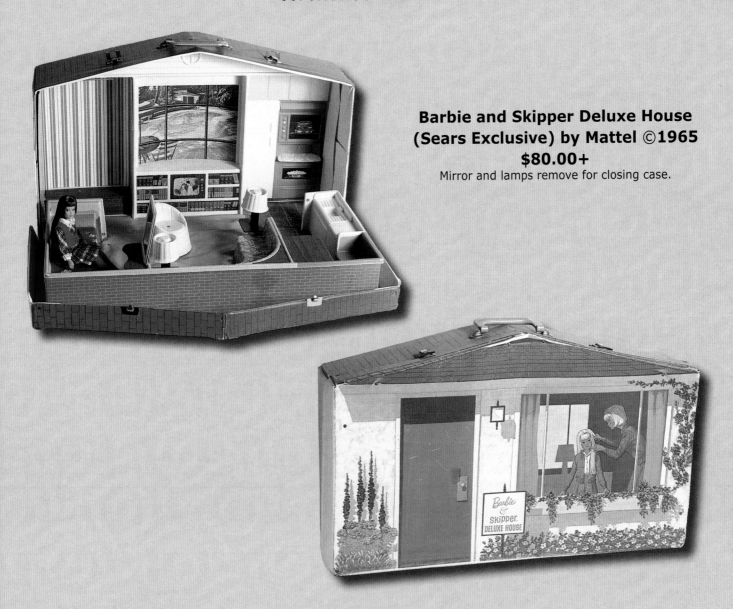

**Barbie and Skipper Deluxe House
(Sears Exclusive) by Mattel ©1965
$80.00+**
Mirror and lamps remove for closing case.

# Bibliography

*Barbie Bazaar, Special Edition.* Mattel and Christmas Catalog Reprints, 1969 – 1972. Murat Caviale, Inc.: Kenosha, WI, 1992)

*Barbie Bazaar, Special Edition II.* Mattel and Christmas Catalog Reprints of Barbie Doll, 1959 – 1965. Murat Caviale, Inc.: Kenosha, WI, 1994)

Deutsch, Stefanie. *Barbie — The First 30 Years, 1959 through 1989.* (Collector Books: Paducah, KY, 1996)

DeWein, Sibyl and Joan Ashabraner. *The Collector's Encyclopedia of Barbie Dolls and Collectibles* (Collector Books: Paducah, KY, 1977)

Eames, Sarah Sink. *Barbie Doll Fashion, Vol. I, 1959 – 1967.* (Collector Books: Paducah, KY, 1990)

Eames, Sarah Sink. *Barbie Doll Fashion, Vol. II, 1968 – 1974.* (Collector Books: Paducah, KY, 1997)

Manos, Paris and Susan. *The World of Barbie Dolls.* (Collector Books: Paducah, KY, 1983)

Pilkenton, Linda. *Skipper Fashion Value Guide, 1964 – 1976* (Sandra Bryan: Austin, TX, 1990)

# Index

# Index

# Index

# Index

# Index

## Chapter 8 Licensed Products